MW00679938

2002

# STRATEGIES *of* REMEMBRANCE

**Studies in Rhetoric/Communication**

*Thomas W. Benson, Series Editor*

# STRATEGIES *of* REMEMBRANCE

## The Rhetorical Dimensions of National Identity Construction

## M. Lane Bruner

University of South Carolina Press

© 2002 University of South Carolina

Published in Columbia, South Carolina, by the
University of South Carolina Press

Manufactured in the United States of America

06  05  04  03  02    5  4  3  2  1

**Library of Congress Cataloging-in-Publication Data**

Bruner, Michael Lane.
  Strategies of remembrance : the rhetorical dimensions of national identity
construction / Michael Lane Bruner.
     p. cm. — (Studies in rhetoric/communication)
  Includes bibliographical references and index.
  ISBN 1-57003-469-9 (cloth : alk. paper)
  1. Nationalism.  2. National characteristics—Political aspects.  3. Political
culture—Germany (West)  4. Democracy—Russia (Federation)  5. Ethno
psychology—Political aspects.  6. Political culture—Québec (Province) I.
Title.  II. Series.
  JC311.B789 2002
  306.2—dc21                                                    2002008028

To the memory of Professor Ernst Behler

To diagnose the particular situation and prescribe the best course of action for a man or a state under given conditions, as a doctor does for his patient, is, as Protagoras saw it, the task of the Sophist. To ensure that that course is followed is the concern of the rhetorician.

W. K. C. Guthrie, The Sophists

# CONTENTS

# SERIES EDITOR'S PREFACE

In *Strategies of Remembrance*, M. Lane Bruner explores the implications of viewing national identities not as facts of nature but as products of rhetorical invention. In recent decades a diverse body of theoretical and historical scholarship has argued that national identity is a symbolic construct. This work has been paralleled and supported by rapidly growing lines of scholarly literature investigating public memory, identity, and community—projects to which rhetorical scholars have made significant contributions.

M. Lane Bruner here presents a comparative rhetorical study of the discourse of national identity in West Germany, Russia, and Quebec. Bruner acknowledges that national identities are deeply embedded in the material infrastructures and the institutional arrangements of societies; at the same time, he argues, these identities are also fictions, always subject to contesting rhetorical appeals. The national identities that are so contested and constructed have the capacity to advance or retard democratic institutions, and crucially affect relations within and between states.

Bruner's account of recent critical moments in the creation of West German, Russian, and Canadian collective identities shows that public discourse was hard at work forgetting and obscuring historical memories, even as it constructed public memory. Bruner argues that such forgetting and such constructing can have real consequences, and provides a convincing case that detailed rhetorical study can support the search for healthy and humane standards for debating national identity.

THOMAS W. BENSON

# PREFACE

This project is the result of a convergence in my graduate studies of rhetorical and critical theories dealing with persuasion, identity, and collective identity construction. Intrigued by the fact that state leaders can be removed from office for publicly proclaiming broadly acknowledged facts—and can also, more obviously, maintain political power by articulating convenient fictions—and given my constant concern that the insights of critical and rhetorical theory be artfully applied to practical civic affairs, investigating the process of national identity construction seemed a useful attempt at better understanding the complex and profound relationship between the ways people talk and the communities they create. This book, an exploration of the public articulation of national identity construction in 1988 West Germany, 1993 Russia, and 1995 Canada, is the result.

To even the most casual observer of world affairs, national identity remains a powerful political force, as witnessed at the close of the twentieth century in the former territories of Yugoslavia and the Soviet Union. Indeed, it is a force that plays a role in one form or another in every state on the planet. Because national identity continues to play such a central role in state affairs, better understanding the process of national identity construction is crucial for those hoping to respond wisely to the unfolding character of the global community. The three examples of the discursive and political battles over national identity provided here are typical of the process and provide a conceptual framework that can be used by anyone seeking to analyze the rhetorical dimensions of nation building anywhere.

Little did I realize, at the outset of this project, how a responsible investigation into the rhetorical dimensions of national identity construction would necessarily involve a broad range of disciplines, including economics, history, international relations, philosophy, political science, and sociology. Nation building takes place not only rhetorically, through the clash of public discourses, but also legally, through constitution building; language and immigration laws; international agreements; rules for citizenship; and laws concerning individual, collective, and corporate rights. It takes place culturally through the construction of public memories, dominant ideologies, popular cultures, literary and artistic traditions, and educational systems. It takes place ethnically through the construction of imagined communities based on physical and/or genetic traits; and it takes place economically through financial systems, economic policies, and the institutional infrastructures supporting those systems and policies. Scholars in many of these areas had already tackled national identity from their unique disciplinary perspectives in ways that were relevant to my own enterprise. However, no one had looked at the phenomenon rhetorically: no one looked at how all of these legal, cultural, ethnic, and economic elements are translated into public discourses where visions of national identity are articulated.

Because of the wide range of scholarship available on national identity, it was challenging to maintain a rhetorical focus. At times this meant going into more detail about relevant rhetoric scholarship than might appeal to a wider readership while cursorily summarizing the broader contexts provided in other fields. However, I hope that balance will please most by better illuminating key interrelationships not featured elsewhere among public discourse, national identity construction, and world order.

This project would not have been possible without the generosity and support of family, friends, and colleagues. Specifically, I would like to acknowledge the generous support of the Babson College Board of Research and the Glavin Center for Entrepreneurial Studies for assistance in the research on Russia (chapter 3). I would also like to acknowledge financial support received from the Center for Advanced Research in the Humanities and the Elizabeth Kerr Macfarlane Endowed Scholarship for the Humanities at the University of Washington for help in completing the studies on Germany (chapter 2) and Canada (chapter 4).

Thanks are also due to the editor of *The Quarterly Journal of Speech* for granting permission to use portions of my essay "Strategies of Remembrance: The (Re)Construction of National Identity in Pre-Unification West Germany," *Quarterly Journal of Speech* 85 (2000): 86–107. I would like to thank the editor of *Javnost/The Public* for permission to use portions of my essay "From Ethnic Nationalism to Strategic Multiculturalism: Shifting Strategies of Remembrance in the Québécois Secessionist Movement," *Javnost/The Public* 4 (1997): 41–57. I would also like to thank the editor of *Discourse and Society* for permission to use portions of my essay "Taming 'Wild' Capitalism," *Discourse and Society* 13 (2002): 167–84.

I would also like to acknowledge, at least in part, the many individuals who made this project possible. First and foremost, I would like to thank Professor Barbara Warnick. John Stewart and John A. Campbell were also keys to the development of the ideas presented here. I would also like to specifically acknowledge my special gratitude to the late Ernst Behler, who, in his beneficent manner, introduced me to the many contemporary European critical theorists who did not always fully recognize that they were rhetorical theorists.

Kate Buckley and Christine Drew, library liaisons at Babson College, also provided key research assistance. My research assistants, Masha Sarakova and Nikolay Belkov, provided invaluable assistance in my Russian work, as did James Janack, Bill Coyle, Dmitry Evstafiev, and the faculty at the School of International Relations at St. Petersburg State University. Andrew King, Edward Schiappa, Carole Blair, Barbara Biesecker, Sue Balter, Brian Seitz, Hazard Adams, and faculty at the University of Illinois, the University of Wisconsin, the University of Pittsburgh, and the University of Massachusetts also provided helpful comments on early iterations of this work. Ultimately, this book is due to the unwavering support of Meryl, my wife. Finally, my warm thanks to Thomas Benson, Barry Blose, the reviewers of early drafts of this manuscript, Scott Evan Burgess, Skot Garrick, and the editorial staff at the University of South Carolina Press for their diligence in shepherding this manuscript into your hands. Any remaining errors are my own.

# CHAPTER ONE

# The Rhetorical Dimensions
# of National Identity

Nations do not have stable or natural identities. Instead, national identity is incessantly negotiated through discourse. What the nation is at any given moment for any given individual depends on the narrative accounts and arguments they bring to bear on the subject. These characterizations vary widely from state to state and from political group to political group and have radically unequal effects on cultures, institutions, economic policies, and laws. Tensions prompted by changes in economic conditions, state authority, real or imagined domestic and international threats, and/or significant changes in cultural markers of national belonging continually cause new groups to become alienated from dominant characterizations of collective belonging, preventing the process of national identity construction from ever being completed.

There is, therefore, a never-ending and politically consequential rhetorical struggle over national identity, and, because national identities are incessantly negotiated, nation building continually requires the services of advocates offering accounts of national character. State representatives and those who publicly contend with them compete for the national imagination of citizens, particularly in times of social unrest, by appropriating available cultural materials to create visions of public belonging. They artfully (and not so artfully) appropriate history and stress economic, civic, cultural, and ethnic dimensions differently for a variety of purposes.

Because characterizations of national identity have various effects on human community, the services of rhetorical critics are also required. Given our historical role as physicians of the state and of human character, rhetoricians are broadly familiar with the various means by which discourses influence communities. Drawing on theories related to persuasion and identity, questions of concern to rhetoricians would include the following: How are different types of national identities generated? What are the constraints imposed on those who speak on behalf of the nation? What or who is omitted from widely accepted conceptualizations of the national character, and what are the material consequences of those omissions? What are the "healthiest" articulations of national character in a given case? Such questions are important, for as Erik Ringmar has observed, "The conception of a community makes a certain kind of person possible, and the conception of a person makes a certain kind of community possible. How we re-present our community also determines who can represent it in the sense of 'standing for it,' 'speaking in its name.' Each re-presentation will make certain kinds of political representation possible and others impossible."[1] It is arguably nothing less than the character of nations, ultimately, that guides the development of economic, cultural, and civic state policies, which in turn influence the trajectory of international relations and world history.

However, central as national identities are to the unfolding geopolitical world order, the rhetorical dimensions of national identity construction remain relatively obscure.[2] While there are numerous studies providing theories and histories of nationalism and while almost all scholars recognize the essential role of discourse in the construction of collective identity, analyses of their actual articulation are rare.[3] Although the role of discourse in the construction of identity has been thoroughly explored theoretically in recent years and the phenomenon of national identity in particular has been analyzed from a variety of scholarly perspectives, comparative analyses of contemporary examples of national identity construction do not exist.[4] To remedy this absence, the goal here is to analyze recent examples of the public articulation of national identity in West Germany, Russia, and Quebec from a rhetorical perspective.

The rhetorical dimensions of national identity are politically significant because different types of collective identities lead to different forms of community. International relations theorist Rodney Bruce Hall notes that "change in the international system occurs with changes in the collective identity of crucial social actors who collectively constitute the units from which the system is comprised."[5] Different national identities lead to different interstate (and intrastate) relations. If West Germans collectively imagine that any surviving National Socialists are now East German communists, then they will view capitalism quite differently from East Germans, who imagine that any surviving National Socialists are now capitalists in West Germany. If citizens of Quebec view themselves as colonized descendants of the New French, then they will treat their federal agreements differently than if they imagine themselves as citizens of a bilingual and multicultural Canada. If Russians imagine themselves as historically repressed democrats, then they will consider Western economic reforms in a manner quite distinct from Russians who imagine themselves as anticapitalist defenders of socialism.

Some characterizations of national identity and the rhetoric that supports them tend to foster democratic communities based on rights, laws, and duties negotiated by a wide range of relatively well-informed citizens. Other characterizations tend to foster authoritarian communities based on xenophobic patterns of identification, the suppression of important historical and political realities, and the maintenance of asymmetrical forms of state power.[6] While there are as many variations on the themes as there are states and while individual states are constantly transformed through discourse, the distinctions indeed make a real political difference. Here, therefore, much of the task will be to isolate unfolding characterizations of national identity, to identify any suppression of important historical and political realities, and to explore the potential social and political implications of those characterizations.

There are several premises guiding the approach to national identity construction taken here. First, national identities are not only assumed to be expressed concretely in property, institutional infrastructures, economic policies, and laws; but they are also assumed to be malleable fictions, assembled out of available historical resources and incessantly negotiated between state and public representatives offering competing accounts of national character. Second, controversial public speeches articulating national character are taken to be useful sites for analyzing the rhetorical strategies involved in competing characterizations of the nation or the people. Third, different strategies of remembrance (politicized forms of public memory) are thought to have different consequences for the character of nations and the quality of international relations.[7]

Fourth, strategies of remembrance have both unique and universal dimensions. On the one hand, strategies are unique in their form and function, directing the critic's focus both toward and away from public discourse. They can become highly complex, particularly in countries with considerable public discourse coupled with a seriously motivated repression—as with Germany and the repression of National Socialism—requiring the critic to engage in close textual analysis to determine the subtle nuances of a developed set of strategies. At other times, as with Russia, the public sphere is so underdeveloped that strategies become the simple and blunt instruments of naked political power. Then the focus tends to be on the nuances of the political context more than on the nuances of the discursive strategies. On the other hand, rhetorical strategies are universally situated in historical, legal, cultural, ethnic, and economic contexts. The critic must always, therefore, thoroughly examine those contexts to fully appreciate the unique functions of competing strategies. Having identified the functions, critics are better positioned to critique the strategies and their likely impact on state formation and international arrangements.

In support of these premises, chapters 2 through 4 analyze the recent public articulation of national identity in three states: West Germany from 1985 to 1988, in the years leading up to the fall of the Berlin Wall; Russia after the collapse of the Soviet Union and during its transition from a planned economy to a market economy in the early 1990s; and Quebec during the vote for independence from Canada in 1995. Together, they support the claim that national identities are based on characterizations that serve widely different purposes and have serious political consequences.

To frame these studies, the following is a brief overview of the history of national identity that introduces its economic, cultural, civic, and ethnic dimensions, followed by an equally brief summary of relevant theories related to the approach taken here to national identity construction. This is not intended as an exhaustive account of the history of nationalism or identity theory, tasks adequately dealt with elsewhere. The goal is simply to introduce readers to the general perspective that guides the case studies.[8] The chapter then concludes with an introduction to the studies themselves. Each is ultimately based on the analysis of controversial speeches related to national identity delivered by state leaders and the public responses to those speeches within the given state's unique historical/political context. By identifying competing narrative accounts within their historical/political contexts, different strategies of remembrance are identified and critiqued.

## *The Emergence of National Identity and Its Various Dimensions*

The emergence of national identities and the globalization of the nation-state system were the result of a number of complex factors. The rise of representative government and industrial capitalism, imperialism and colonialism, the territorial identification that accompanied the expansion and development of state bureaucracies and official state languages, defensive reactions of local elites to the encroachments of interstate commerce, and romantic nostalgia for quickly evaporating folk cultures each played a role.[9] Territorial-sovereign states, ruled by monarchs whose legitimacy was derived from "divine right" and whose relative worldly status depended in large part on the development of trade, eventually gave way to national-sovereign states governed by thriving merchant classes whose legitimacy depended on the production of national identities.[10] State leaders were increasingly compelled to consolidate local economic and cultural resources to defend themselves against more economically developed states. Simultaneously, merchants began investing in the states.[11] These events initially led to a number of progressive social policies pursued by monarchs who recognized the value of securing the general welfare and approbation of subjects, particularly as a counterweight to the rising influence of the propertied classes, and later included progressive social democratic policies such as Franklin Roosevelt's New Deal. The economic nation, therefore, was the product of a wide range of state policies, from protective tariffs to social security, designed to protect the interests and secure the allegiance of subjects. This, in turn, led to greater public identification with the state.[12]

While early forms of state identification began to emerge in the monarchial states of Europe several centuries ago, it was the nineteenth and twentieth centuries that witnessed the global triumph of the nation-state principle.[13] The collapse of the Ottoman and Austro-Hungarian empires, the retreat of military colonial powers, the creation of the League of Nations and the United Nations, and the later dissolution of Yugoslavia and the Soviet Union further instantiated the nation-state principle.[14] The idea that states represent nations has justified a variety of foreign policy measures in the United States since at least the time of Woodrow Wilson; and by the dawn of the twenty-first century, the primary public justification for the construction of new sovereign states was the declared need to protect a historically oppressed people.

Just who these oppressed people are at any given moment in time, however, is not only an economic relation but also a rhetorical construction, and dominant characterizations of nations have life-and-death consequences for the "peoples" of the world. Simply comparing the estimated eight thousand spoken languages and the real and imagined histories of those who speak them to the two hundred odd states currently in existence shows us that not all potential "peoples" enjoy "self-rule." Instead, as Ernest Gellner has observed, most linguistic groups "go meekly to their doom . . . dissolving into the wider culture of some new national state."[15] Conversely, it is equally clear that the steady fragmentation of the globe into smaller and smaller "national" units could easily continue for some time, given the rich linguistic and cultural resources still to be mined from humankind.

An important corollary of the economic nation is the *cultural* nation, which is composed of folk, ethnic, and civic elements. Subjects of states reap the benefits and suffer the consequences of economic policies differently, and most are unaware of those policies; whereas the cultural dimensions of a nation are generally shared. Citizenship usually requires that subjects speak the nation's language, obey the nation's laws, honor the nation's traditions, "believe in" the nation, and be willing to make personal sacrifices on behalf of the nation. In addition to these cultural and civic markers, in some states citizenship remains openly based on ethnic criteria, and those failing to meet those criteria are de facto aliens.[16]

Most of these cultural, civic, and ethnic conceptions of national identity were not possible before the rise of economic nationalism, the expansion of the bureaucratic state, and the development of official state languages. For example, universal literacy, enabled by state-provided education, had profound effects on increasingly urbanized workers who, having been drawn to industrial centers from rural regions, found themselves thrown into relatively anonymous and impersonal societies.[17] Local forms of identity based primarily on interpersonal relationships were irreversibly transformed through the acquisition of official state languages and participation in collective state institutions such as public schools and conscripted armies. By the middle of the nineteenth century, this gradual transformation from preliterate and interpersonal forms of community to literate and imaginary institutional forms of community, coupled with the progressive distribution of wealth and privileges to state-educated workers, led to increasing identification with the state.

The operations of the global economy, the rise of state bureaucracies, the development of state languages, and urbanization have shaped, and continue to shape, national identities. Furthermore, the various historical and economic paths taken by different states have resulted in the creation of national identities with widely different cultural, civic, and ethnic components.[18] Civic nations are based on narratives that justify the construction of a political community with common institutions, rule of law, a bounded territory, and a sense of legal solidarity. Ethnic-cultural nations, conversely, are based on narratives that emphasize shared historical memories, myths of common ancestry, rule by law, and a sense of ethnic or cultural solidarity.[19] While each nation's ever-unfolding identity is composed of some unique combination of these economic, cultural, civic, and ethnic elements, all are based on discursive accounts of who "the people" are and the place of "the nation" in the world. It is here that rhetorical theories related to the construction of publics, as well as critical theories related to the social construction of identity, are helpful.

### Mapping Strategies of Remembrance

Collective identities are negotiated through the clash of multiple and conflicting discourses, including battles over memory, over domestic and foreign policy, and over constitutions and the meaning of laws. State and public representatives provide accounts of national character, but only particular kinds of accounts are consistent with the imagined communities preferred by publics. There are more and less popular national characterizations—and many fail dramatically—but competition over national identity is a permanent feature of domestic politics.

A national identity is not simply a narrative or set of narratives that subsequently prompts and justifies a wide range of actions; it is also an ongoing rhetorical process.[20] Accordingly, the rhetorical approach adopted here is designed, not to uncover *the* identity of a nation, but to analyze moments in time when competing articulations collide in the ongoing discursive negotiation of what it imaginatively means to be a member of a nation. The approach is based in part on Friedrich Nietzsche's theory of history, Michel Foucault's notion of a limit attitude (an ethic of permanent resistance against the limits imposed by consensus), and Ernesto Laclau and Chantal Mouffe's notions of hegemony and radical democracy.[21] Within this rhetorical-philosophical framework, collective identities are assumed to be political inasmuch as they are always a choice between narratives; and while subjects are never hostage to the effects of a single narrative or identity (e.g., national identity), it is nevertheless the case that many particularly influential narratives entail politically consequential exclusions oftentimes invisible to those who identify with them.[22]

This theoretical approach is based on the analysis of controversial discourse, for it is through transgressions, or resistance, that the "limits" of identity are revealed.[23] The approach can perhaps best be understood as a response to William Connolly's plea for an "agonistic ethic" in which "people strive to interrogate exclusions built into . . . entrenched identities."[24] It is an attitude toward consensus based on the assumption that all forms of identification and the narratives that accompany them simultaneously create a field of absence, an Other, and/or forms of forgetfulness, and that only through a reflective appreciation of these limits can the emancipatory potential of collective identity by maximized. As a critical rhetorical approach, it seeks to identify narrative limits and the absences/omissions they entail, which in turn makes them available for emancipatory purposes. As a method, it is the contextual analysis of controversial speech.[25]

The analysis of controversial public discourse in West Germany reveals that the articulation of national identity was based on the rhetorical strategy of identifying West Germans as "victims" of National Socialism and erasing National Socialist perpetrators from public memory. In Russia it was based on the strategy of identifying Yeltsin and his economic policies with "democracy," coupled with erasing from public memory the lingering influence of the collapsed Soviet system and the general absence of democratic features such as compromise, the separation and balance of political power, and the institutional infrastruc-tures required for effective competition. And in Quebec the public articulation of national identity was based on the strategy of "multiculturalism" and the era-sure from public memory of ethnic/cultural motives for secession, when in fact, the historical motivation for Quebec secession had always been based on the protection of French Canadien culture from English Canadian hegemony.

Nietzsche informs this approach by distinguishing among three types of his-tory: monumental, antiquarian, and critical. Those who engage in *monumental history* construct a past "worthy of imitating" and "use history as an incentive to action."[26] Such use of the past is always "in danger of being somewhat distorted, of being reinterpreted according to aesthetic criteria and so brought closer to a fiction."[27] State and public leaders, eager to acquire or maintain a general con-sensus among citizens in order to gain compliance in relation to the exercise of the means of violence, monumentalize history in order to interpellate the "ideal citizen."[28] Those who engage in *antiquarian history* supposedly love history for history's sake and wish to preserve it rather than use it. Antiquarian history is perhaps best described as the pure chronological record (e.g., at what time a person arrived, the clothes he was wearing, what she said, etc.). Even antiquar-ian histories, however, are highly selective, for it is impossible to record every possible detail relevant to a given historical event. *Critical history*, finally, relates to those who critique monumental and antiquarian histories in order to right perceived injustices in how and what they exclude.

Competing characterizations of national identity, according to such a scheme, constitute battlegrounds of interests. State and public leaders, intent on fabricating a commonly held account of who are "the people" that can be called upon in times of crisis to mobilize publics, engage in monumental his-tory to suppress contradictory aspects of a nation's history and to create wide-spread support for preferred policies. These monumental histories are likely to be more pernicious than the less politically motivated antiquarian histories, and we have only chronological records (and personal memories) with which to compare those monumental histories for their veracity. Though all identities have a fictional dimension, relatively accurate antiquarian histories do quite well is revealing the significant historical absences required of monumental histories.

The approach used here functions as critical history inasmuch as it isolates dominant articulations of national identity and the narrative omissions they entail in order to make them available for reflection.[29] By contextually analyz-ing controversial public speeches, critics can determine more precisely the kind of national identity being constructed in a given state and significant things that cannot be said lest the narrative account unravel. Initially, the rhetorical critic identifies a controversial speech or speeches disseminated in some form to a nationwide audience.[30] The speech or speeches should include an articulation of what it means to be a citizen of the given state, who "the people" are, or what the state stands for and should provoke a broad spectrum of negative reactions. Then, by analyzing these reactions, the critic seeks to identify patterns of responses to the speeches, paying particular attention to the discourse cited as being especially offensive. Reasons usually accompany such reactions, and patterns of reasons constitute competing accounts of the nation's character and help to reveal the "unspeakable" in a given monumental history. After having simultaneously explored the relevant historical, economic, cultural, ethnic, and legal contexts for those addresses and responses, strategies of remembrance and their functions can be mapped.

## Strategic Memory in West Germany, Russia, and Quebec

No history can be a completely honest history. All concepts, all identities, and all narratives necessarily leave out many things. This is not to say, however, that all are equally dishonest or that they leave equally important things out. It is to say, instead, that characterizations of national identity can be distinguished by what they do not say; and the following studies show that recent characterizations of national identity in West Germany, Russia, and Quebec were indeed accompanied by very different kinds of politically significant absences. As noted, in West Germany those absences concerned the causes for, continuities of, and responsibility for, National Socialism. In Russia those absences related to the general lack of concrete democratic processes, the battles over state power and economic control in the wake of the Soviet collapse, and how those battles influenced the construction of the new Russian constitution. And in Quebec those absences centered on an ethnic nationalism that had outlived its usefulness.

Chapter 2 examines how state leaders in West Germany and the United States characterized the German people as victims rather than perpetrators of the Second World War. The dominant characterization was that the West German nation had suddenly become "democratic" at the end of the Second World War. The fascist roots of the German state were displaced onto communist East Germany, and the remembrance of the Holocaust was turned into an exercise in forgetfulness and forgiveness. Chapter 3 discusses the construction of the post-Soviet Russian constitution, and how the dominant characterization of both the legislative and executive branches of government was that they alone were "truly democratic." In fact, neither branch was particularly democratic. The struggle for power between the executive and legislative branches, which itself mirrored the federal struggle between the center and the periphery and between the "Russian" regions and the "ethnic" republics, was actually the main issue during the construction of the constitution. Chapter 4 examines how the *"peuple Québécois,"* historically characterized as French Canadien, were recharacterized as a multicultural people. Even though the main purpose behind secession was purportedly to protect French-Canadien culture from dissolving into English Canada, that purpose failed to inspire a large enough percentage of the population to secure Quebec's independence. Therefore, there was a shift in strategy from ethnic nationalism to civic multiculturalism.[31]

The studies collectively show that national identity is indeed the ever-changing product of a constant rhetorical struggle in which different factions use history in different ways to achieve different ends. Ronald Reagan, Helmut Kohl, and Richard von Weizsäcker characterized the German people as victims in order to dissociate fascism from "democratic capitalism" and to erase the memory of the perpetrators of National Socialist crimes. George Bush, Bill Clinton, and Boris Yeltsin each characterized Russia as a democracy. However, behind the democratic discourse was a concerted effort not to create a viable constitutional democracy based on a clear balance and separation of powers, but to ensure that certain market reforms were implemented and that a "strong" presidency be constitutionally established. Jacques Parizeau and Lucien Bouchard characterized the people of Quebec as the descendants of the New French because historically the French Canadians have called for secession in order to protect their culture. Lucien Bouchard, however, recognizing that secession would not be possible without a new strategy, embarked on an incompatible path of strategic multiculturalism to persuade a larger number of people to identify with the state in order to achieve greater economic leverage within the federation.

All in all, the three studies show how varied, how politically consequential, and how potentially dangerous are the rhetorical games that surround the construction of national character and how they influence economic policies, laws, and forms of imagined community. They show that characterizations of both one's own nation and other nations shift with time and circumstance and that the process continues unabated. They also suggest that similar studies could be done of any state, especially when an advocate characterizes the people in a way that is dramatically rejected.

This is a start. Since it is unlikely that national identities are going away any time soon, it is in our best interest to understand as fully as possible how they are articulated through public discourse. The analysis of controversial speech is a fruitful approach to that task.

# CHAPTER TWO

# National Identity in
# Pre-Unification West Germany

The profound social and political consequences of national identity have perhaps been most dramatically witnessed in Germany. Devastated by the military defeats of the twentieth century, Germany has experienced a persistent identity crisis throughout its recent history.[1] The surrender of the National Socialists at the end of World War II led to nothing less than the geographic division of the German state, the forced division of German citizens into "democratic" West Germans and "communist" East Germans, and the difficult division between younger (innocent) and older (guilty) Germans. For West German leaders in the years leading up to the reunification of East and West Germany, characterizing the nation was treacherous business along a precipitous route. Those engaging in commemorative public discourse had to speak very carefully, for any characterization of German identity was forced to stand in the long and dark shadow of the horrors of National Socialism and ethnic nationalism.

One controversial speech in particular helps to elucidate the strategies of remembrance governing national identity construction in the years leading up to German reunification: Philipp Jenninger's commemoration of the fiftieth anniversary of the *Kristallnacht*, a euphemism for the dramatic escalation of physical violence perpetrated against German Jews on 9 November, 1938 (the term "night of crystal" referring to broken glass from Jewish-owned property). The speech was truly a dramatic failure and thus serves as an appropriate site for the identification of strategic memory. The speech triggered an avalanche of negative responses in the German press because it transgressed the limits of the dominant strategy of remembrance as expressed two and a half years earlier by German President Richard von Weizsäcker.

On the morning of 10 November, 1988, Bundestag President Jenninger learned just how delicate the relationship between German national identity and National Socialism was when he addressed the West German parliament and selected guests commemorating the *Kristallnacht*. In his speech, Jenninger attempted to explain why the German people were drawn toward National Socialism, stressing Germany's responsibility for crimes against the Jews and the necessity of directly confronting Germany's Nazi past. While from an outsider's perspective such an explanation might appear relatively uncontroversial, for his German audience it certainly was not. Only moments into the address, members of the audience began heckling Jenninger, and by the end of the speech more than fifty parliamentarians had walked out and another had been removed by force.[2] In the days that followed, German newspapers uniformly attacked Jenninger, claiming he had "distorted German history" and had attempted to "justify" Hitler. Accused of tactlessness and lack of historical understanding, if not of outright sympathy for Hitler himself, Jenninger was forced to resign the following day, leading many to the realization that aspects of Germany's National Socialist past still could not be publicly discussed. But what was it, exactly, that could not be publicly discussed? And why?

### Bitburg and the Historikerstreit: West German Remembrance of National Socialism

Two historical events in the years leading up to reunification illustrate the problematic relationship between West German national identity and National Socialism and help to explain why Jenninger's address was so controversial. The first is President Ronald Reagan's decision in 1985 to participate with West German Chancellor Helmut Kohl in ceremonies at Bitburg, Germany, marking the fortieth anniversary of Germany's surrender at the end of World War II. The controversies surrounding Reagan's decision to visit a German cemetery containing graves of SS soldiers help to illustrate important ideological issues related to the remembrance of National Socialism. The second event is the *Historikerstreit*, or "debate between the historians," that erupted in the West German press one year later. This important and long-lasting public debate was fundamentally concerned with the role that the remembrance of National Socialism should play in the reconstruction of German national identity. Together, these events shed significant light on what was at stake when the relationship between national identity and National Socialism was publicly addressed in West Germany and illuminate the "negotiated" character of West German national identity in the years leading up to German reunification. Specifically, the discursive events comprising the Bitburg visit and the *Historikerstreit* reveal various narrative limits placed on West German government representatives and help to explain both the failure and the success of speeches delivered by West Germany's conservative leaders during that period.[3]

It was the commemorative events related to Reagan's visit to Bitburg that set the tone for the remembrance of National Socialism and the public negotiation of national identity in the years leading up to the reunification of Germany.[4] The characterizations offered by Reagan mirrored the characterizations

later offered by West German President Richard von Weizsäcker when the ceremonies culminated in his highly praised speech to the Bundestag on 8 May,
1985.[5] Three days earlier, Reagan and Kohl laid wreaths at Bergen-Belsen concentration camp (after the site was cleared of Jewish protesters), then traveled
to Kolmeshöhe military cemetery in Bitburg where Kohl gave an address (a few
SS soldiers were buried there). Both men then proceeded to the U.S. Air Force
base nearby where Reagan gave a short speech.[6]

The function of the commemorative events was complex. According to
Geoff Eley, "for Helmut Kohl and his advisors, the Bitburg event was to complete Germany's post-war rehabilitation: commemorating Europe's liberation
from Germany was turned into Germany's liberation from its past."[7] Harvard
historian Charles Maier concurs with Eley's claim, arguing that "for Chancellor Kohl and his political advisors, the American president's visit was intended
symbolically to wipe away the last moral residues of probation under which the
Federal Republic still labored."[8]

Reagan and his advisors had other reasons for participating in the commemorative events. Stephen Brockmann maintains that Reagan's motive for
participating at Bitburg was primarily "to construct a history useful to Cold
War ideology."[9] And Kathryn M. Olson notes that Reagan "seemed motivated
by gratitude to Kohl for being the European point player in favor of deploying
Pershing 2 and cruise missiles. Reagan further appeared to be currying West
German support for his space-based missile defense plan and for American
involvement in Nicaragua. Finally, there was the administration's more gen-
eralized desire to strengthen U.S.–W. German diplomatic relations."[10] Additionally, the United States government was attempting to maintain the cultivated image of West Germany as a democratic ally in the fight against communism. According to Brockmann, the U.S. government, in part through its
"reeducation programs" at the end of the Second World War and its aborted
denazification policies, worked to construct a political fiction, or "mytholo-
gized history," whereby Nazi (West) Germany was "magically" transformed
into a stable and happy democracy: "According to Allied decree in 1945, the
German Reich had ceased to exist, and as it was decreed so it came to pass.
Suddenly there was no more German Reich, and there were no more Nazis,
and the United States began to use the services of those who had ceased to be
Nazis in the continued fight against communism, the new Nazism." Significantly, according to Brockmann, "this magical transformation is possible only
if Nazism is ignored."[11]

Exemplifying this erasure of National Socialists were statements made by
Reagan before his visit to Germany. For instance, on 21 March, 1985, Reagan

claimed that "none of them [the West German people] who were adults and participated in any way [in World War II] are still alive, and very few . . . even remember the war."[12] Of course, such a statement was absurd in 1985, when thousands of former Nazi soldiers and functionaries would have been about as old as Reagan himself was. Nonetheless, Reagan's statement articulated a vision of West Germany as being "Nazi free." Another telling remark was Reagan's statement on 18 April, 1985, when he stated that "there's nothing wrong with visiting that cemetery where those young [SS] men are victims of Nazism also. . . . They were victims, just as surely as the victims in the concentration camps."[13]

If Brockmann is correct, (and many scholars agree with him), West Germans, prompted in part by U.S. policies, had built "a wall of silence" around themselves in relation to their National Socialist past.[14] Furthermore, events and statements from the chronological historical record suggest that this wall of silence was patrolled by at least two general principles related to public discourse dealing with National Socialism and German nationalism. First, any public acknowledgment of West German responsibility for National Socialist crimes would be problematic because the "success" of the West German image depended on a forced forgetfulness and silence in relation to Nazism for both the Kohl and the Reagan administrations. To acknowledge the existence of perpetrators in West Germany was to work against the narrative that the Nazis had magically been transformed into good democrats. Second, if political leaders were to deal with National Socialism at all, they would have to be extremely careful not to blame West Germans. Instead, they would have to focus on the "victims."[15] The principal reason that the focus would have to be on the victims rather than the perpetrators was the fiction that there were no more perpetrators left to address.

While the Bitburg ceremonies suggest the ways in which the remembrance of National Socialism could be used for international ideological maneuvering, the *Historikerstreit* was more concerned with battles between political factions over how national identity should be constructed within West Germany. Whereas Bitburg revealed that the "West German miracle [was] dependent not on transformation but on the erasure of memory,"[16] the *Historikerstreit* revealed how that forgetfulness could be used for other more specific intra-national political purposes.

The "debate between the historians" was fundamentally a prolonged public struggle in the German press between journalists, historians, and philosophers arguing for different forms of national identity. One of the two general camps engaged in this debate reflected the so-called *Tendenzwende*, or the conservative turn in German historiography represented by advocates like Ernst Nolte, Michael Stürmer, Joachim Fest, and Andreas Hillgruber. This group held that it was the job of historians and public officials to construct a strong, "conventional" national identity, which, coincidentally, required a "normalization" of the National Socialist period.[17] Additionally, they argued that critical historiography and international pressures, such as globalization, were dangerously undermining Germany's national pride and thereby the state's political/hegemonic base. Also, they wanted to please the West in order to maintain West Germany's international standing as a "reliable" member of NATO.[18] The second camp, opposing the "conservative" historians, was composed of "critical" historians like Jürgen Habermas, Hans Mommsen, Jürgen Kocka, and Heinrich August Winkler. Predominantly, members of the "critical" camp were concerned about the "packaging" of history by conservative historians, the importance of "learning from history," and the importance of promoting civic/constitutional rather than ethnic/cultural national identity.[19]

Exemplifying the conservative position was Michael Stürmer, a former advisor to Kohl. He argued for the construction of a "more positive" view of German history and an overhaul of the West German educational system in order to achieve that view.[20] Eley points out that Stürmer wanted to present a view of German history fundamentally without Nazism, for "only by circumventing Nazism [could] the historic bases of national identity be regained . . . and [unless the circumvention was accomplished] the German 'guilt-obsession' [would] continue to block a more balanced approach to the national past."[21] Stürmer maintained that the government should play an active role in creating a sense of conventional/cultural national pride, and he stated that "the search for a lost past is not an abstract striving for culture and education. It is morally legitimate and politically necessary. We are dealing with the inner continuity of the German republic and its predictability in foreign policy terms."[22] "In a land without history," Stürmer warned, "the future is won by those who are able to harness memory, coin concepts, and interpret the past."[23]

The political leaders of the Christian Democratic Union (CDU) such as Weiszäcker and Kohl generally shared Stürmer's views. For example, a campaign speech by CDU presidential candidate Joseph Strauss in January of 1987 called for "a purified national consciousness," because "German history cannot be presented as an endless chain of mistakes and crime, and our youth thereby robbed of the chance to recover some genuine backbone."[24] Kohl followed a similar rhetorical strategy, stating that "whoever steals the younger generation's historical understanding also steals the future."[25]

In the *Historikerstreit*, then, and in the political discourse of the CDU, conservatives appear to have engaged in the following strategy of remembrance. In order to maintain the narrative that Nazis had suddenly become good democrats, and in order to allow young Germans to (re)construct "cultural" nationalism, the National Socialist period had to be minimized. Guilt over National Socialism was undermining a "healthy" national consciousness. CDU politicians generally managed the strategy by maintaining a repentant public posture, avoiding any explicit discussions of the causes or consequences of National Socialism, dissociating themselves from the National Socialist era, apologizing on commemorative occasions related to the Nazi era (particularly the Holocaust), and focusing primarily, if not solely, on the "victims."

For the opposition, such a strategy was unacceptable. Habermas asserted that Stürmer and other conservative historians and politicians were working for a revisionist history in the service of a nationalist renovation of conventional (noncivic) identity. As a critical historian, Habermas offered another strategy: a defense of "constitutional patriotism" and "post-conventional" (civic) identity.[26] As opposed to the traditional German notion of cultural/ethnic nationalism, perhaps most famously represented by the philosophy of Johann Herder (without the chauvinism of National Socialism), constitutional patriotism (civic nationalism) is based on allegiance to just laws rather than to cultural or ethnic affiliations. Habermas was concerned about the ways in which conservatives were attempting, in his opinion, to create an ideological climate, in the service of capitalism, built upon a purely "conventional" identity.

The conservative historian Nolte was adamantly against any vague notion of "post-conventional" identity, which he associated with the rise of capitalism *and* communism, the loss of cultural affiliation, and the atomization of society. Conservatives, then, believed they were protecting West German citizens from cultural atomization in the service of capitalism and/or communism. Critics, conversely, were attacking cultural nationalism because of its association with chauvinism and the tendency of the state to use noncivic forms of identity to further its own political aims.

Defenders of both the conservative and critical positions passionately attempted to protect the social values they held most dear; and embedded within the struggle between traditional, conventional, cultural identity and post-conventional identity based on "constitutional patriotism" were the various ways in which history was selectively appropriated by both sides. Both the conservatives and their critics were, albeit in very different ways, "packaging" history. According to Elizabeth Domansky, "the Left and the Right argue their respective positions within radically different frameworks, but they both dehistoricize the Third Reich by only accepting for themselves and for Germany selected parts of Germany's history during those twelve years. In fundamentally different and yet very similar ways, the Left and the Right have again met in the effort to repress memory."[27] Brockmann perhaps best explains the primary reason why the National Socialist period had to be repressed by representatives of both the conservatives and their critics (or those defending and those attacking the Reagan/Kohl style of market democracy):

> It is not a coincidence that the dominant ideologies of both the Western and Eastern power blocks are incapable of dealing with the reality of fascism, for fascism as a third element necessarily destroys the symmetry of the ideological bipolar opposition. Hence Western ideologists [e.g., Kohl and Reagan] must view fascism as a kind of socialism (emphasis on National *Socialism*), a totalitarianism essentially equivalent to Soviet Communism, and Eastern ideologists [e.g., official historians of East Germany and to some extent the critics of the Kohl and Reagan governments] must view fascism as a kind of capitalism, the desperate ploy of bourgeois capitalism *in extremis* (emphasis on *National* Socialism). For each, fascism becomes a kind of metaphor for the ideological Other.[28]

Therefore, anyone attempting to "explain" National Socialism would at the same time be making some kind of ideological judgment along one of these two lines, and any explanation of the National Socialist era would be a controversial one. To borrow Domansky's words, within West Germany the narrative of the conservatives was that "West Germany remembers and rejects the Holocaust" (thus dumping all remembrance of National Socialism into the Holocaust and allowing the remnants of fascism within West German capitalism to go unexamined), while the narrative of critics was that "the West German Left resists the recurrence of fascism" (thus allowing the critical historians to dissociate themselves from any traces of the fascist legacy within West Germany's capitalist democracy while simultaneously implying that conservative leaders were defenders of capitalist/fascists).[29] Responsibility for fascism, then, was avoided altogether.

Before looking closely at the public speeches by Weizsäcker and Jenninger and how those speeches articulated two very different visions of national identity, a brief summary of the constraints on public discourse suggested by the various narrative positions assumed by the conservatives and their critics during Bitburg and the *Historikerstreit* is in order. For Germany's *conservatives*, to maintain a "healthy national consciousness," public commemorative discourse related to National Socialism would likely be expected: (1) not to discuss, but to condemn, the National Socialist period; (2) not to discuss the perpetrators of National Socialist crimes, but to focus on the victims (for there were no more perpetrators); and (3) not to directly accuse the West German people as a whole, but to find a way to praise German character despite the unfortunate past (because the ultimate goal of commemorative discourse was to rebuild a conventional national identity).

The basic strategy of remembrance for the conservatives' *critics* during this period required that public commemorative discourse: (1) never associate the conservatives' critics with the perpetrators (because they are, in fact, the resistance); (2) avoid attempts to "explain" National Socialism (because any explanation could be easily used by conservatives as a tool for minimization and/or justification); (3) follow any mention of the National Socialist period with immediate condemnation and dismissal, especially since cultural/ethnic nationalism is directly opposed to constitutional/civic patriotism; (4) focus on the victims unless accusing the elder representatives of the conservatives, because they were the "real" perpetrators, and the victims should be given voice; and (5) find a way to praise the new German democracy (because the ultimate goal of commemorative discourse was to strengthen the liberal traditions embedded—although not necessarily promoted—within the capitalist system).

In sum, both conservatives and their critics agreed that National Socialism had to be dealt with very carefully. It was therefore almost impossible for a public speaker to successfully negotiate these constraints, for any attempt to discuss the National Socialist period would likely transgress the limits imposed by the various strategies of remembrance. The challenges presented by such a difficult negotiation suggest why Weizsäcker's speech was so universally admired, since it "played by the rules" so artfully, and why Jenninger's speech was such a disaster, since it appears to have disregarded these rules altogether.

### Richard von Weizsäcker: Remembrance for Reunification

By far the most successful commemorative address in West Germany between the years 1985 and 1988 was President Richard von Weizsäcker's speech at the end of the ceremonies commemorating the fortieth anniversary of the end of the war in Europe. Delivered to the German parliament on 8 May, 1985, almost a year before the eruption of the debate between the historians, the address served as a culmination to the events commemorating V-E Day. Critics across the board in the German press praised the speech, arguing that

Weizsäcker had broken new ground by publicly acknowledging the criminality of the Nazi regime.[30] However, it was also the case that Weizsäcker's speech was successful, not because it encouraged a direct investigation into the causes and continuities of National Socialism, but because it encouraged a form of remembrance ultimately in the service of forgetfulness. While Weizsäcker's speech was considered by many West Germans to be an exemplary model by which other commemorative addresses could be compared, the address was successful at a certain price, for as Domansky has noted, "Weizsäcker . . . never challenged [the] new avoidance strategy of his country in his much acclaimed speeches, but rather expressed it quite beautifully."[31]

Although the government had announced that the slogan for the events related to Weizsäcker's address would be "Freedom or Totalitarianism," a slogan that allowed the government to avoid the use of the term "National Socialism" and at the same time to vaguely suggest that the choice was actually between capitalism-as-freedom and fascism-as-communism,[32] accounts from representatives of both camps claimed that Weizsäcker dealt "effectively" with National Socialism. Even Habermas, a longtime critic of the conservative CDU government, stated that "[Weizsäcker's] address to the parliament . . . strikes me as one of the few political speeches that does justice to the demands made on us by twelve years of Nazi rule and the forty years since."[33] Saul Friedländer, another staunch critic of Germany's "struggles with memory," argued that "Richard von Weizsäcker [did] not avoid a detailed enumeration of Nazi crimes and stressed, with great sincerity and courage, the central place of the destruction of the Jewish people in Nazi ideology and practice. For the Western reader, Weizsäcker's address is an exemplary admission of the utter criminality of the Nazi state."[34] Timothy Ash, another of Kohl's critics, stated that Weizsäcker's speech was "magnificent" and that "the problem of guilt was . . . addressed in an exemplary fashion."[35] Such comments, especially coming from those normally critical of conservative policies and public addresses, point to how "successful" the address actually was.

Weizsäcker's address focused on two central themes: the importance of looking at "truth without distortion" and the importance of focusing on the "victims" of National Socialism. After the perfunctory salutations, Weizsäcker stated, "We [Germans] must find our own standards. We are not assisted in this task if others or we spare our feelings. We need and have the strength to look truth straight in the eye—without embellishment and without distortion." Immediately following these words, he added, "For us, the 8th of May is above all a date to remember what people had to suffer."[36] Therefore, from the very beginning of the address, Weizsäcker engaged in what could be read as a significant incompatibility. As the following excerpts indicate, although he stated that he would "look truth straight in the eye" and "without distortion," Weizsäcker's address associated the National Socialist period with the victims (those who suffered) rather than with the perpetrators (those who caused the suffering). By focusing on the "victims," he managed to avoid any significant discussion of responsibility for the suffering caused by the German people (reducing responsibility for the crimes to Hitler and "a few people"), and instead, confused the suffering Germans *caused* with the suffering they endured as a result of National Socialism.

After reiterating the importance of "undistorted truth" and a sole focus on "victimage," the second section of Weizsäcker's speech consisted of a lengthy list of the various "victims," which included the "dead of the war," "the six million Jews who were murdered in the concentration camps," "all nations who suffered in the war (including the Soviet Union and Poland)," and "German compatriots who died as soldiers (or during air raids at home, in captivity or during expulsion)."[37] Also, Weizsäcker included widows, homosexuals, gypsies, members of the resistance, and those who suffered "because of fear of death and arrest . . . and grief over everything which [they] had wrongly believed in and hoped for." This passage was sophisticated in that it helped to identify a wide number of groups who could think of themselves as victims of National Socialism. Weizsäcker broke new ground by acknowledging the suffering of women, communists, Polish émigrés, and homosexuals. Usually West German remembrance of National Socialism had been limited to Germans and Jews, so Weizsäcker not only expanded the number of victims (thus widening the base of identification) but also simultaneously managed to place side by side the suffering of "all nations" and "six million Jews" with the suffering of "German compatriots." This move, mirroring Reagan's, helped to "magically" turn perpetrators into victims.

After establishing the broad base of victims, the next section of the speech consisted of a series of statements seeking to minimize the active participation of the German people in National Socialism and at the same time stress the "unspeakable" nature of the Holocaust. That is, while the previous section sought to identify and level the broad field of victims, this one sought to minimize and dismiss the field of perpetrators. Weizsäcker claimed: "At the root of the tyranny was Hitler's immeasurable hatred against our Jewish compatriots"; "The perpetration of this crime [the Holocaust] was in the hands of a few people"; "There were many ways of not burdening one's conscience, of shunning responsibility, looking away, keeping mum"; and "Everyone who directly experienced that era should today quietly ask himself about his involvement then."[38] Granted, these statements were nestled among numerous phrases claiming that all of the German people were affected by the consequences of the Holocaust and that remembrance is crucial, but nonetheless, underlying these phrases was a subtle subtext. Fundamentally, Weizsäcker was saying that National Socialism can be reduced to the Holocaust, that the Holocaust can be reduced to Hitler and "a few people," and that others were simply guilty of a passive, rather than an active role in National Socialist crimes.[39] By asking those in the audience who might have been guilty to "quietly ask themselves" about their involvement, Weizsäcker suggests that judgments of guilt (and responsibility) should be "quiet" and personal, not "loud" and public.

The middle sections of the speech enumerated a number of factors mitigating the responsibility of the German people for the war and identified the German people as its ultimate victims. Weizsäcker stated that "the 8th of May marks a deep cut not only in German history but in the history of Europe as a whole. The European civil war had come to an end, the old world of Europe lay in ruins." "Along the road to disaster Hitler became the driving force. He whipped up and exploited mass hysteria. A weak democracy was incapable of stopping him. And even the powers of Western Europe—in Churchill's judgment unsuspecting but not without guilt—contributed through their weakness to this fateful trend." He recounted that "the Soviet Union signed a non-aggression pact . . . [which] allowed Hitler an opportunity to invade Poland. The Soviet leaders at the time were fully aware of this. And all who understood politics realized that the implications of the German-Soviet pact were Hitler's invasion of Poland and hence the Second World War." But after all of the statements indicating that the Second World War was a "civil war" basically caused by Hitler, the weakness of England, and the opportunism of the Soviet Union (rather than primarily a result of the rampant chauvinist ethnic nationalism of the German people), Weizsäcker asserted that "[These things do] not mitigate Germany's responsibility for the outbreak of the Second World War."[40] Weizsäcker concluded, "At the end of it all only one nation remained to be tormented, enslaved, and defiled: the German nation."[41]

With the West German public now characterized as the "tormented and defiled nation" who had been fooled by Hitler and condemned by a weak England and an opportunistic Soviet Union, Weizsäcker then telegraphed the ultimate subject of his speech: divided Germany. After asserting that the Germans "became victims of [their] own war," he quoted East Berlin's Cardinal Meissner saying, "The pathetic result of sin is always division."[42] The introduction of the theme of "division" led Weizsäcker into the final sections of his speech where he addressed the German people's sadness over the loss of German territory (both East Germany and sections of Poland), the importance of promoting peace, elaborate praise for the "lessons learned" by the West German government, and, finally, a call for German reunification. Having established that Germany had "learned its lessons," Weizsäcker concluded his speech with an explicit call for reunification, thus completing the transformation of a speech commemorating the defeat of National Socialism into a speech calling for the reunification of Germany.

> Forty years after the end of the war, the German people remain divided. . . . We Germans are one people and one nation. We feel that we belong together because we have lived through the same past. We also experienced the 8th of May 1945 as part of the common fate of our nation, which unites us. . . . The people of Germany are united in desiring a peace that encompasses justice and human rights for all peoples, including our own. Reconciliation that transcends boundaries cannot be provided by a walled Europe, but only by a continent that removes the divisive elements from its borders.[43]

In this remarkable passage, Weizsäcker provided the conclusion for the syllogism that the previous excerpts suggest framed his address: The German people must remember National Socialism (as the Holocaust, causally reduced to Hitler and other countries, and not really reflective of the German people in general, who are the ultimate victims) in order for there to be "proper" reconciliation. "Proper" reconciliation meant a reunified Germany. Therefore the German people must remember National Socialism (and simultaneously forget about the causes and continuities of fascism) in order to reunify Germany. So in the end, the purpose of remembrance was not to uncover the causes of National Socialism; not to try to understand why so many German citizens allowed, promoted, or actively supported the various crimes against humanity perpetrated by the National Socialist regime; and not to reveal the dangers of cultural/ethnic nationalism. Rather, Weizsäcker sought to remember in order for the German public to forget and be forgiven.

It is not surprising, therefore, that Weizsäcker's speech was a tremendous success. Not only did it manage to turn the commemoration of the end of National Socialist tyranny into a call for German reunification, but at the same time it appeared to expand the limits previously constraining the remembrance of National Socialism. Weizsäcker publicly proclaimed Germany's guilt (although his proclamations were always preceded by statements of minimization) and also broke new ground in expanding the publicly acknowledged field of "victims." Less noticeable was Weizsäcker's smooth blending of the victimized and the victimizer, which provided deserved absolution for younger Germans while simultaneously stifling public critique of older Germans less deserving of absolution.

Most important, Weizsäcker managed to articulate a German identity that resonated with the strategies of remembrance constraining West German public discourse. In following the strategies of remembrance of the conservatives, Weizsäcker: (1) minimized the number of perpetrators of National Socialist crimes and managed to avoid any significant discussion of those crimes (despite claims to the contrary); (2) predominantly focused on the "victims;" and (3) found a way to praise the German people. In following the strategies of remembrance of the conservatives' critics, Weizsäcker: (1) avoided placing any broad blame on the German people as perpetrators; (2) called for reunification with East Germany and peace with the "Eastern neighbors," thus avoiding any overt scapegoating of the Left; (3) made no serious attempt at "explaining" National Socialism; (4) focused on the "victims" in an artful and thorough way; and (5) found a way to praise the new German democracy and the liberal traditions embedded within the capitalist system.

All in all, Weizsäcker appears to have done everything "right," not only by working with (if not helping to further develop) West German strategies of remembrance but also by artfully turning an event commemorating National Socialist tyranny into an instrument for reunification. Whatever the potential positive and negative consequences of his characterization of German identity and its contribution to West German identity management, it provided a model by which the subsequent address of Philipp Jenninger would be judged, an address that articulated a completely different vision of what it meant to be "German" in the years just before reunification.

### The Dramatic "Failure" of Jenninger's Kristallnacht Address: Problematizing Remembrance

In contrast to Weizsäcker's dramatically "successful" speech, by far the most infamous and unsuccessful commemorative address in West Germany in the years immediately preceding German reunification was Philipp Jenninger's *Kristallnacht* address.[44] Just as Weizsäcker's address met with nearly universal praise in Germany, Jenninger's address met with nearly universal condemnation. Representative of many of the parliamentarians present for the address, Berlin's Federal Democratic Party (FDP) deputy Wolfgang Leuder argued that Jenninger had "laid the foundation for a false understanding of history by the Germans," had disregarded "the necessary degree of dismay for the victims of the National-Socialist terror [and had] avoided only a few historical mistakes."[45] Hubert Kleinert, the Greens' parliamentary whip, said that the speech was "embarrassing, verging on the tasteless [and] the most shameful event he had seen in parliament."[46] German newspapers, as well as most major newspapers from around the world, uniformly attacked Jenninger in the days following the address, some going so far as to proclaim that Jenninger had engaged in "Hitler worship,"[47] while others negatively compared Jenninger's speech to Weizsäcker's.[48]

According to several observers, there really was not much that was *factually* untrue in the address, but almost everyone thought it to be *inappropriate* both in style and content.[49] It is this disparity between the content of Jenninger's address (an explanation of the causes of National Socialism, detailed descriptions of its criminal nature, and a call for West Germans to stop repressing their National Socialist past) and its reception (that Jenninger attempted to "justify" National Socialism, provided a "false understanding" of German history, and showed "insufficient sympathy for the victims") that is the focus here, first through a discussion of Jenninger's style and delivery, and finally through a discussion of Jenninger's "failure" to remember strategically.

Perhaps the finest critiques of Jenninger's style are provided by Thomas B. Farrell and Peter Polenz—critiques that provide useful starting points for an investigation into the reasons why Jenninger's speech was so dramatically rejected.[50] Farrell, fundamentally from an Aristotelian/Habermasian perspective, focuses on Jenninger as the speaker/agent and on the "monumental impropriety" of Jenninger's address.[51] He points out how Jenninger's choice of words seemed to implicate every German as a perpetrator and how "the events [related to the Holocaust], in their very enormity, [were] too close to their audience to permit space for reflection and eventual renewal."[52] After noting the fundamental historical accuracy of Jenninger's speech, Farrell argues that Jenninger's style was too confrontational (an "epochal taunt"),[53] that Jenninger "may have abandoned more direct, reflective address prematurely, without even having given it a fair chance," and in doing so, failed to provide the audience with the opportunity to be "witnesses to, and judges of, their own role in history."[54]

Farrell's analysis is well supported when one reads the opening sections of Jenninger's speech. Jenninger began his lengthy address (over 7000 words) by stating, "Today Jews in Germany and everywhere in the world are thinking back to the events that took place fifty years ago. We Germans, too, recall what happened."[55] At least one critic in West Germany noted that this separation of "Germans" and "Jews" was inappropriate at commemorative occasions because it implied a division between Germans and Jews.[56] Even more problematically, Jenninger immediately expanded on his initial division by explicitly stating that the Jews were victims (uncontroversial enough), and by implying that the West Germans, as the collective addressees of the speech, were perpetrators (controversial indeed!). Specifically, Jenninger stated, "Today, we are meeting in the German Bundestag to remember the pogroms of November 9 and 10, 1938— since not the victims, but we, in whose midst the crimes occurred, need to remember and account for what happened: since we Germans want to clear our minds in relation to our understanding of history and with regard to lessons for the political structuring of our present and future."[57] Since one of the dominant strategies of remembrance in West Germany was to minimize the association of being German with being a perpetrator (if not to avoid discussing perpetrators altogether), Jenninger's phrase "not the victims, but we" was a direct challenge to accepted convention. Since there were no more perpetrators, Jenninger, in effect, was speaking to a group that (fictionally) no longer existed. As Jenninger's opening remarks revealed, he was going to speak as a representative of the perpetrators, and it was at this early point in the address that audience members began heckling him.

Jenninger's problems quickly multiplied in subsequent sections of his speech, where he "confessed" that most of the German public during the Second World War had willingly engaged in criminal behavior, or at least had passively stood by. Here Jenninger confused the dominant strategy of minimization of responsibility with admissions of more widespread guilt. Initially, Jenninger mirrored Weizsäcker by stating that "the violence involved [in the *Kristallnacht*] was not a manifestation of spontaneous mass anger, whatever the motivation may have been. Instead, it was a measure planned, instigated, and promoted by the government."[58] Sentences later Jenninger added, "Only very few people joined in the violence," but then he tempered his minimization with "everyone saw what was happening, but most people looked the other way and remained silent. The churches also remained silent."[59] Yet even this "confession" continued the process of minimization, à la Weizsäcker, as it reduced the complicity of the average German citizen to a passive silence rather than an active and complicit role in the segregation of, and violence against, the Jews.

To this point in the address, Jenninger, although on treacherous ground because of his distinction between "the victims" and "the Germans," had managed to avoid any concrete discussion of the perpetrators. But in the following section, Jenninger begins to seriously confuse the code of minimization by not only directly speaking of the perpetrators but actually quoting from a conversation between two particularly infamous Nazis: Hermann Göring and Joseph

Goebbels. Jenninger, quoting Göring in relation to the *Kristallnacht*, states, "I would have preferred it if you had killed two hundred Jews and had not destroyed so much valuable property."[60] The use of direct quotes and indirect speech (stylistic choices repeated throughout Jenninger's speech) were perhaps the most problematic stylistic aspects of the address, especially in the sections where Jenninger moved back and forth between direct quotes, indirect speech, rhetorical questions, and speaking in "his own" voice.

There are two primary reasons why these stylistic strategies created problems: Jenninger's delivery was very poor, and he failed to provide sufficient textual and vocal cues for the audience to be able to easily "read" the speech.[61] In an article critiquing the style of Jenninger's address, Polenz provides various reasons for Jenninger's problems in this area. First, in quoting others in the German language, one should use the subjunctive form in order to indicate that one is "distancing oneself" from what is being said, something that Jenninger did not do. Second, according to Polenz, because *the stylistic codes related to the remembrance of National Socialism are so well established*, speakers deviating from those codes need to provide constant commentary so that audiences will know what is going on.[62] Third, the use of indirect speech is a rather sophisticated literary device unfamiliar to many of the parliamentarians, and is especially hard to "read" without appropriate shifts in voice.

Since Jenninger made frequent use of quotations and indirect speech throughout the address, these problems were magnified as the speech continued. Concerning the lack of "distance" shown by Jenninger, individuals were quoted using the simple past instead of the subjunctive form. While in English there are no substantial differences between the two forms, in German there is. As an example, one could say *"Er sagte das Hitler ein guter Führer ist"* or *"Er sagte das Hitler ein guter Führer sei"* (both of which roughly translate into English as 'He said Hitler was a good leader'). The former sentence uses the simple past and is read by German audiences as a more or less factual statement, while the latter sentence uses the subjunctive form, which the audience interprets as merely the reported (and perhaps dubious) opinion of someone else. Jenninger's failure to use the subjunctive form provided some in his audience, as well as numerous critics, with the opportunity to question the nature of Jenninger's own attitude toward the attitudes and opinions reflected in the quotes. Nevertheless, as Polenz notes, the more profound reason for the confusion was that the West German people had so deeply routinized public discourse related to National Socialism that the codes had become dangerously banal, and that the antecedent forms were so deeply ingrained in German consciousness that any deviation had to be accompanied by considerable commentary.[63] These deep routines, these antecedent forms, suggested but not sufficiently explicated by Polenz, I maintain, are strategies of remembrance.

Jenninger's style, then, contributed to the ultimate rejection of his address. The early sections established three dangerous precedents: he would speak to the audience as if they were perpetrators (or at least nonvictims); he would quote and indirectly speak from the perspective of the perpetrators without providing sufficient vocal and/or textual cues; and he would confusingly combine strategies of remembrance (thereby irritating both conservative and oppositional government representatives). The content of the speech was not factually untrue or purposefully misleading, but the dominant strategies of remembrance (in both style and content) were deeply ingrained in the public's consciousness and the imagined community was narratively constrained. The public so "filtered" Jenninger's discourse that any explanation was viewed as justification, and the notion that the German people en masse had been perpetrators was viewed as a "distortion" of German history.

Jenninger's address is saturated with instances where the strategies of remembrance are mangled, but a few representative instances should suffice to establish that claim. In an early section of the speech, Jenninger stated, "Looking back it becomes clear . . . that in actual fact between 1933 and 1938 a revolution took place in Germany—a revolution in which a system of government based on the rule of law was transformed into a system of government based on injustice and criminal acts."[64] Recall that one strategy of remembrance allows those critical of the conservative stance to dissociate themselves completely from any responsibility for National Socialism because, they argue, conservatives choose to repress National Socialism. Therefore, the task of uncovering structural and political continuities between German history, National Socialism, and West German capitalism falls to the opposition. In this section, Jenninger controversially (for anti-conservatives) suggested that the National Socialist period was an aberration in German history rather than a result of deeper social continuities.

To make matters worse, in a later section of the speech, Jenninger engaged in an extended discussion of Hitler that suggested, among other things, that there *were* deep continuities between German history and National Socialism. Jenninger stated that "Hitler's so-called 'worldview' lacked anything in the way of original thinking. Everything had been there before him: hatred of the Jews developed to the point of biological racism, emotional resistance to things modern."[65] Not only did Jenninger contradict an earlier statement that Jews enjoyed equal status before 1933, but he also contradicted the conservative fiction mentioned earlier that National Socialism was an aberration caused by Hitler and a handful of his henchmen.

Other examples, and perhaps most damaging for Jenninger, were the long, detailed descriptions of Nazi atrocities toward the end of his address: detailed descriptions of the mass shooting of Jews (including women and children) from the perspective of the perpetrators. Here Jenninger forced his audience members to assume the subject position of the perpetrators, and this was something probably no one in the audience was willing to do. The first lengthy quote is from an eyewitness who explains how entire Jewish families stripped, lined up, comforted one another, and then were shot by SS soldiers who were casually sitting around smoking cigarettes and laughing and chatting between rounds of shooting. In the second lengthy quote, Heinrich Himmler tells SS troops that the ability to kill Jews in cold blood was a "difficult task" required out of "love [for] our people." At the end of these accounts, Jenninger concluded, "These sentences leave us with a sense of helplessness, just as the millions of deaths leave us feeling helpless. Numbers and words do not help. The human suffering involved cannot be made good. And every individual who became a victim was irreplaceable for his loved ones. Thus, something remains for which all attempts to explain and understand fail."[66] Such a conclusion would seem unsatisfactory for a number of reasons. Just as Weizsäcker had stated that the crimes were "unspeakable," Jenninger stated that words "do not help." Members of the opposition could be offended, not only because Jenninger failed to adamantly condemn these long passages but also, as was reflected in the *Historikerstreit*, many critical philosophers and historians feel that only through a continual confrontation with the past (directed at conservatives) is national identity in Germany sufficiently problematized. To say that words do not help could be viewed as being tantamount to dismissing the debate and analysis altogether. For conservatives, such long passages explicitly transgress the sanction against publicly discussing National Socialist crimes—and if "words do not help," then why bother?

The conclusion of Jenninger's speech will serve as a final example of the numerous ways in which Jenninger confused strategies of remembrance. He begins by refocusing on "confession" and "admission of guilt" and how the West German public, after acknowledging their guilt, could play a new moral role in international affairs. Here Jenninger states that there were "many Germans [who] let themselves be blinded and led astray by National Socialism," but that young Germans want to accept the past without distortion because "self-liberation in confrontation with horror is less torturous than repressing it."[67] And he concludes his speech with a plea to his audience: "Ladies and

Gentlemen, keeping remembrance alive and accepting the past as a part of our identity as Germans—this alone promises both us members of the older generation as well as members of the younger generation liberation from the burden of history."[68] Here Jenninger unwittingly contradicted the full force of West Germany's avoidance strategies and thereby sealed his political fate (his removal from office and retirement from politics), since almost all of the fictions constructed around the remembrance of National Socialism and the fabrication of West German national identity were designed precisely *not* to keep remembrance alive.

As the above examples indicate, Jenninger "failed" in a wide variety of ways. Not only was his delivery poor, his stylistic moves questionable, and his speech logically confused, he also transgressed each and every established strategy of remembrance. As far as conservatives were concerned, Jenninger: (1) concretely discussed the National Socialist period and suggested that the causes of National Socialism could be traced to continuities within German society, implying the Nazis were not an "aberration" in German history; (2) did not immediately condemn and dismiss the National Socialists and failed to provide the required "commentary" and "distance"; (3) focused on the perpetrators rather than the "victims"; and (4) never found a way to adequately praise the German people. As far as the opposition was concerned, Jenninger broke all of their rules as well: (1) he lumped the entire audience (save for the younger generations) together as perpetrators; (2) he attempted to "explain" National Socialism (which is tantamount to justification); (3) he failed to provide sufficient commentary on the perspective of the perpetrators, therefore insufficiently condemning and dismissing the National Socialist period; and (4) he was unable to find a way to praise the new German democracy but suggested instead that the West German public was still in denial.

Ultimately, Jenninger lacked Weizsäcker's "art." Nonetheless, as the above analysis suggests, Weizsäcker's "success" and "artfulness" depended on an articulation whereby German soldiers were equal to concentration camp victims and where the average German citizen's participation in National Socialism was reduced to a passive silence. Jenninger's "failure," conversely, was based on his insistence that West Germans directly confront the average German citizen's active and passive complicity in National Socialist crimes. Yes, it was confused, stylistically problematic, and poorly delivered; but at no point did Jenninger engage in "Hitler worship," nor could he be reasonably accused of providing a "misleading" account of German history. Rather, Jenninger's speech appears to have unintentionally transgressed the limits imposed on public discourse in the years leading up to Germany's reunification.

## German Amnesia and the Critique of Narrative Omissions

Germany is unique, and the German struggle for national pride and unity is obstructed by a tragic history. Since chauvinistic national pride and racist ethnic unity led to the horrors of the Second World War and the Holocaust, it is hardly surprising that the German people would have a difficult time articulating their national identity in ethnic or cultural terms. Another aspect of the West German situation that distinguishes it from the Russian and Canadian studies that follow is that the controversies surrounding the public negotiation of national identity were unrelated to constitutional controversies but were triggered instead by commemorative events. Since a constitution was forced upon the West Germans at the end of World War II, and since the state had done so well economically in the intervening years, the constitution itself was not at issue.

As the following cases suggest, in states where the basic law of the country is being negotiated, national identity becomes highly contested. Germany's uniquely difficult state history, however, especially the virulent ethnic nationalism of the National Socialist period, apparently leads the German people to constantly battle with themselves over their national identity, in contrast to states where identity battles are usually triggered by dramatic changes in the political or economic climate.

Despite its unique characteristics, articulations of national identity in West Germany, as in Russia and Canada, were accompanied by politically consequential narrative omissions. In general, public discourse was guided by the absence of National Socialist perpetrators as well as by a variety of "substrategies" derived from this primary absence. Perhaps due to the intense repression of the Nazi era, coupled with a relatively developed public sphere, the strategies became quite complex in the years before reunification. Consequently, no public forum could contain forthright discussions of the causes, consequences, and possible continuities of fascism in Germany without the displacement of blame.

Stated more broadly, the West German case reveals how publics can identify with narratives that have the potential, as Kenneth Burke noted, to deflect attention from crucial sociopolitical realities.[69] For scholars interested in what Stephen H. Browne refers to as "the politics of public memory," the isolation of *specific* absences through the analysis of dramatically rejected speech arguably marks an important step forward in the critique of publics. Browne points out that "forgetting is itself integral to the work of public memory" and that memory "is more likely to be activated by contestation, and amnesia is more likely to be induced by the desire for reconciliation."[70] West German public discourse in the years leading up to reunification directly supports such claims, revealing as well how specific narrative absences (amnesias) can be identified through the analysis of dramatically rejected discourse. By isolating specific omissions, critics are able to identify more precisely what is being forgotten and in turn begin to critically evaluate the kinds of political work being done by public memory.

But one pressing question remains: How are we to evaluate these narrative absences, these politically consequential omissions? If articulations of collective identity are always selective and forgetfulness is integral to the work of public memory, how are we to distinguish a necessary absence from an egregious one? From the perspective of a critical historian, an egregious absence might best be described as one that is politically motivated in such a way as to preclude reflexive public discussion of crucial sociopolitical issues, suppress the development of just institutions, and/or redirect wealth in socially harmful ways. Such criteria are based on an ethic that values a maximally informed citizenry as well as on the assumption that publics are usually in various states of disinformation and cannot necessarily be presumed "reasonable."

Were the absences related to West German national identity egregious? Did attempts by public officials to erase the perpetrators of National Socialism from public memory constitute the kind of absence that would preclude healthy public debate? The near-universal praise for Weizsäcker and disdain for Jenninger suggests that the West German public identified themselves as victims, not perpetrators, thus contributing to a politics of memory that elided serious public discussions of responsibility for National Socialism. To that extent, monumental history succeeded. Nevertheless, the *Historikerstreit* also showed that West Germans were willing and able to publicly question this absence, albeit it in a way that projected responsibility onto the Other. Perhaps attempts such as Jenninger's to salvage a morally tenable national identity in Germany are doomed to fail until enough time has passed that all the perpetrators have *really* died and the present fiction becomes a reality.

# CHAPTER THREE

# The Discourse of Democracy
# in Post-Communist Russia

Two years after Jenninger's *Kristallnacht* address, the Berlin Wall fell. Jenninger was out of politics, and Weizsäcker's plea for reunification had been answered: East and West Germany were no more. Simultaneously, other momentous transformations in the nation state system were taking place to the east. The Soviet Union, the last of the great multinational empires, was collapsing; and in the aftermath of that collapse, the citizens of states such as Armenia, Georgia, and Lithuania, reveling in their newfound freedom, were busy with the chaotic and sometimes violent process of nation building.

For Russians, however, "independence from the Soviet Union" created as much of an identity crisis as an identity opportunity, for they paradoxically had declared independence from themselves by turning away from an identity cultivated for over seventy years: the Soviet identity.[1] Historically an undemocratic, multicultural, and anticapitalist state ruled by czars and Communist Party bosses, deprived of the benefits of a healthy civic culture, torn by purges and revolutions, vacillating between an envy of the West and a hatred for the West, and now stripped of its Soviet identity, Russia was a country whose national identity was difficult to predict.

But there would be dramatic transformations. On 12 June, 1990, the Russian Soviet Federated Socialist Republic officially declared sovereignty from the Soviet Union; and one year later, for the first time in their history, Russians went to the polls and elected a president: Boris Yeltsin. As the candidate of the "Democratic Russia" party, Yeltsin's election held promise for the development of unprecedented liberal economic and political reforms in the formerly communist country. Championed as an undaunted defender of democracy in the West, he publicly declared his determination to steer Russia away from its Soviet past and into the happier waters of "free markets and democracy." But it would be rough sailing. Between 1991 and 1993, although Russia was the site of unprecedented civic freedom, politicians battled with increasing ferocity over the pace and direction of economic and constitutional reform. While they wrangled, average citizens suffered. Inflation soared to over 2,400 percent. Savings and pensions evaporated. Public services were dismantled. Health care became scarce except in major cities, and the life expectancy for Russian males dropped rapidly, from 63 to 57 years.[2] Behind these sad facts and behind the scenes of the public political battles, the formerly state-controlled natural and financial wealth of the country settled into the corrupt hands of colluding business "oligarchs" and local and federal government officials.[3]

In the midst of this social disaster, contending politicians argued that Russia could only become a *true* democracy if their version of economic reform and their draft of the constitution were adopted.[4] In oftentimes carnivalesque public spectacles, ex-Soviet officials—including industrial oligarchs, military leaders, monarchists, economic neo-liberals, and hard-line communists—all claimed to be the true democrats. Their opponents, each insisted, were mere imposters. In the West, the dominant characterization of the situation was that Yeltsin and the members of the executive branch of government were the true democrats; the rest were imposters. But was that the case?

Answers to these and other questions related to national identity construction in post-Soviet Russia can be found by reviewing three controversial public addresses delivered by Yeltsin between March and October of 1993, at the height of the political battle over the new constitution. Yeltsin, through his public discourse, persuasively characterized Russia as a "democracy" and himself as a "democrat" while simultaneously constructing an authoritarian presidency that, with the support of Western advisors, eventually contributed to the criminalization of Russia.

The first speech, delivered to a statewide audience on 20 March, 1993, was designed to head off legislative attempts to suspend temporary powers granted to Yeltsin during the early transition to "free markets and democracy." Those powers had been granted to help push through unpopular—although considered necessary—economic reforms, such as the privatization of state assets.[5] In light of the social devastation caused by those reforms, however, the legislature had finally decided to act. In response, Yeltsin sought to maintain his exceptional powers by bypassing the legislature and appealing directly to the people for a public vote of confidence for him and for his economic policies.

The second controversial speech, on 5 June, 1993, opened a Constitutional Assembly convened by Yeltsin and his advisors to hammer out a draft of the new constitution based on "presidential power." There he characterized his political opponents as "anti-democratic Bolsheviks," who in turn were associated with the legislative and judicial branches of government. He provided a history of "democratic Russia" interrupted by the Soviet era, concluding that the choice for Russians was ultimately between a constitution proposed by the democratic and progressive executive branch and an antidemocratic Soviet-style constitution proposed by the backward-looking legislative and judicial branches.

For most Western observers, such a characterization of Russia's political situation was anything but controversial. However, in a situation reminiscent of Jenninger's fateful *Kristallnacht* address, the Assembly speech proved highly controversial for Russians, as more than fifty delegates walked out of the address and another was removed by force after attempting to approach the podium. While the protesters' actions were viewed in the West as further proof that hardline communists were still trying to block the development of democracy in Russia, the protesters insisted that Yeltsin was anything but a democrat. Instead, they argued that they were, in fact, the *true* democrats, and that Yeltsin was actually blocking the development of democracy in an attempt to reinstall yet another authoritarian regime in their long-suffering country.

Yeltsin's third and ultimately most controversial speech was delivered on 23 September, 1993, when he finally put an end to the battle over the new constitution by appearing on state television and simply announcing that he was dissolving the "Soviet" legislature and would temporarily rule by decree until elections for a new Congress of People's Deputies and a referendum on the new constitution (both based on his preferred constitutional draft) took place.

All of these speeches created intense public controversy in Russia and therefore serve as appropriate discursive sites for the identification of strategies of remembrance. In each speech Yeltsin consistently maintained that there was a growing crisis between "democratic" reformers such as himself and "Soviets" influencing the other branches of government, and that the crisis was impeding his ability to represent the will of the Russian people and establish a new, truly democratic constitution. His opponents were increasingly outraged. After his March address, Yeltsin was almost impeached (one of many such attempts). After his June address, many of the most influential delegates walked out in protest; and armed conflict broke out in the streets of Moscow after the September address, eventually leading to a military assault on the parliament building.

Despite the negative responses to Yeltsin's addresses in Russia, his extra-constitutional measures (under the existing Soviet-era constitution Yeltsin had no legal right to dissolve parliament) met with praise in the United States, especially after the defeat of the so-called rebellious forces occupying the parliament building following the September address. With the defeat of the opponents of Yeltsin's version of economic and constitutional reform, senior U.S. State Department officials maintained the outcome had vindicated the Clinton administration's belief that Yeltsin had helped turn Russia from communism to democracy.[6] Clinton spoke with Yeltsin by phone after the address and, according to Press Secretary Dee Dee Myers, "felt reassured by the conversation . . .

[for] Yeltsin basically said that obstacles to democracy and [economic] reform had been removed."[7] Strobe Talbott, Clinton's choice as special ambassador for coordinating U.S. policy toward the new states of the former Soviet Union, noted that while Americans were "not in the habit of applauding the suspension of parliaments or constitutions," circumstances in Russia were "exceptional."[8]

Indeed, the circumstances *were* exceptional. Centrifugal tendencies that had undermined the Soviet Union threatened to tear apart the Russian Federation as well, as federation members, following the lead of the autonomous Soviet republics (e.g., Lithuania, Ukraine, Kazakhstan), declared independence and established their own constitutions. Ethnic conflict outside of Russia was widespread as "nations" struggled with one another in the former Soviet territories. An ongoing "war of laws" between the executive and legislative branches of government at both the federal and local levels within Russia was escalating dangerously, and the existing Soviet-era constitution failed to adequately delineate any meaningful separation or balance of powers. Former officials involved in the centralized and militarized Soviet economy continued to have a profound influence on Russian politics and the Russian economy, while radical nationalist and communist voices were reaching larger and larger audiences. In light of the financial stresses caused by the economic reforms that were attempted (e.g., privatization), these factors were magnified. Yeltsin's "extra-constitutional" move, if able to quell the threats to "free markets and democracy" and put a stop to the continuing intransigence of a "reactionary" Congress unwilling to implement "necessary" economic reforms, was viewed as a welcome end to the divisive wrangling.

After all, if anyone in Russia was a democrat, surely it was Yeltsin. In his inaugural address in July 1991, he had proclaimed his appreciation for the fact that the people, in electing him president, had chosen "the path of democracy."[9] Standing bravely on one of the Soviet tanks surrounding the Russian parliament building two months later and calling on the people to rally to the defense of "democratic" Russia, Yeltsin had become a symbol for defiance of the Soviet system. When the tanks finally retreated and Russia's independence was secured, George Bush declared that the events had left "the world looking at [Yeltsin] as a very courageous individual, duly elected by the people, standing firmly and courageously for democracy and freedom."[10] Two years later the "rebellious" parliamentarians and other members of the opposition, occupying that same parliament building in defiance of Yeltsin's decree, became a symbol for the last remnants of the oppressive Soviet system. As Yeltsin's tanks surrounded the building, preparing to forcibly remove his political adversaries, President Clinton, echoing Bush, proclaimed that Russia "had already become a democracy" and that Yeltsin was "a genuine democrat."[11] After the "rebellion" had been crushed and the opposition leaders (e.g., the vice president and the Speaker of the parliament) had been imprisoned, it was only a matter of months before Russia adopted its new constitution. "Democracy" had finally been established in long-suffering Russia.

At least this was the way the situation was dominantly characterized in the United States and in the pro-Yeltsin media in Russia. However, a closer look at the reactions to Yeltsin's speeches during the battle over the Russian constitution reveals a competing—and rather surprising—characterization. Two major Russian newspapers, *Izvestiya* and *Rossijskie Vesti*, fully supported Yeltsin and were in unison with the characterizations coming from the United States. However, not only the more radical presses, such as *Pravda* and *Den'*, but also a number of moderate papers, such as *Nezavisimaia Gazeta*, argued otherwise. There, instead of being championed as the defender of democracy in the months leading up to his September decree, Yeltsin was increasingly accused of having "dictatorial pretensions," was frequently referred to and addressed as "Czar Boris," and was repeatedly characterized as one whose constitutional maneuverings were nothing less than "designs for a coup d'état."

Yeltsin's advocates, conversely, argued that such accusations were predictable, given the sources. Of course the very people with dictatorial intentions— the old Soviet functionaries (*nomenklatura*) in Congress trying to subordinate the executive branch of government to the legislative branch—would accuse the *true* democrats of such intentions.[12] Despite such logic, however, there are reasons other than the perhaps predictable reactions of Yeltsin's opponents to question just how well democracy fared in 1993 Russia. At first glance, it seems paradoxical enough that overpowering the competing branches of government and establishing rule by executive decree would achieve the triumph of democracy. A longer look raises other, less paradoxical reasons for concern. It is a fact that the new constitution adopted in December 1993 bore little resemblance to the one promised by Yeltsin in his opening address to the Constitutional Assembly that June. There, Yeltsin had emphasized the crucial importance of the separation and balance of powers, decentralized federalism, and an independent judiciary. Instead, the new constitution made the president clearly the most powerful figure in the state.[13] While Yeltsin openly preferred a constitution that would strengthen the role of the executive, his apparent willingness to compromise in June faded after the success of his September decree. Critics of Yeltsin prior to his "constitutional coup" argued that, despite his many appeals to freedom and democracy, it was Yeltsin who was attempting to dominate the legislative and judicial branches—a justified claim in light of the new constitution and in light of the "coronation" of Vladimir Putin in 2000.[14] In reacting to Yeltsin's speeches, his political opponents repeatedly declared that *they* were the actual democrats, that Yeltsin was in the back pocket of Western capitalists outside of Russia and industrial oligarchs within, and that only they were truly on the side of the people.

So who were the true democrats? What were the political and economic realities surrounding this "democratic" duel? Why did political leaders focus on the civic and economic dimensions of national identity instead of the ethnic or cultural dimensions? What purposes did democratic discourse serve after the Soviet collapse? What, after all, does a true democracy look like? To investigate these questions and better determine the context for Yeltsin's controversial addresses, it is initially helpful to review how the history of Russian federalism contributed to the post-communist battle over the new constitution, to then review the history of the constitutional battle itself, and finally to survey Yeltsin's addresses and the patterns of responses to those addresses (particularly the address of 20 March). In so doing, the dominant strategy of remembrance at work in 1993 Russia will be clarified, revealing in greater detail how Yeltsin fictionally dissociated himself from the "Soviets" and associated himself instead with the term "democracy" to secure disproportionate power in the executive branch of government, purportedly to overcome "Soviet" resistance to "democratic" reform. That "democratic" reform, however, was only partial; for while the Russian people certainly gained unprecedented civic freedoms by the end of 1993, the economic reforms in the early years of the new Russia and the constitutional reforms implemented in late 1993 ultimately did little to create the kind of "true democracy" promised by Yeltsin. Instead they resulted in the establishment of an authoritarian presidency and the criminal takeover of the natural and financial resources of the country.[15]

### *Russian Federalism and the "Nationalities Problem"*

Unlike the situation in Germany, national identity in Russia has rarely been successfully articulated along ethnic or cultural lines. During the Soviet era, for example, national identity was predominantly expressed in imperial and economic, rather than ethnic or cultural terms (e.g., the Russians are Soviets). Paul Goble asserts that this is because "the Russian state became an empire before the Russians became a nation . . . and Russians were never forced to define what the proper limits of their [ethnic-cultural] identity or their territory should be."[16] This is not to say, however, that ethnic and/or cultural dimensions of Russian national identity do not exist. Edward Walker has properly noted that "being Russian means a great deal to most Russians. The great achievements of Russian culture, and Russia's long and dramatic history, provide . . . a deep reserve of mythology that will help preserve Russian statehood."[17] But ethnic and cultural characterizations of Russian identity were all but absent in post-Soviet public discourse, which focused instead on civic and economic characterizations related to the new constitution and market reforms.

The Soviet identity was fundamentally imperial and economic rather than ethnic or cultural due to at least four key influences: the cultural complexity of the Russian state, Marx's theories of nationalism, Lenin's and Stalin's policies related to the "nationalities problem," and the subsequent federal structure of Russia.[18] The direction of national identity construction in post-communist Russia was framed by these influences. Unlike the case in Germany, where there is basically one state language, or in Canada, where there are two, more than 200 languages are spoken in the Russian Federation, eighteen of which have more than a million speakers; and there are more than 125 different officially recognized cultural groups.[19] To maintain harmony among the diverse cultural and linguistic groups within the empire, ethnic and cultural articulations of national identity have rarely been politically expedient. During the Soviet era, the "workers of the world" were best united in a multicultural socialist struggle against "bourgeois nationalism" and capitalism.[20] The construction of the Soviet identity, while little other than a thinly veiled continuation of czarist attempts at "Russification" (state-sponsored institutions and policies designed to ideologically assimilate non-Russians), exemplifies the tendency of Russians to define themselves, not in overt ethnic or cultural terms, but in multinational and (usually) anti-Western terms.[21]

A second resonant influence working against an explicitly ethnic or cultural national identity in Russia was Marxist theory. While the nineteenth century witnessed the construction of nation-states across Western Europe, Karl Marx viewed national identities as a dangerous bourgeois distraction from the more important category of class.[22] Recognizing the disruptive potential of separatist struggles, however, Lenin and Stalin, despite Marx's theoretical observations, gave a great deal of attention to what they termed the "nationalities problem" and enacted a series of policies designed to fend off potential cultural conflicts.[23]

Initially, both Lenin and Stalin publicly argued in favor of "the self-determination of peoples," basing their arguments on Marx's notion that national identities were the result of capitalism and would dissolve into class identity with the development of socialism. Stalin, for example, wrote *Marxism and Nationalism* in 1913, arguing that every "oppressed nation" should be free to break away from Russia; and Lenin's 1917 *Declaration of the Rights of the Peoples of Russia* explicitly stated that the nations of the Russian Empire were equal and sovereign. According to the *Declaration*, nations were also guaranteed the right to secede as well as the right to cultural development.[24] By the Third Congress of Soviets in January 1918, however, Stalin had changed his mind, and the wording of the *Declaration* was revised so that the right of secession was reserved only for the "toiling masses." This discursive move allowed Soviet authorities to reject all separatist demands as contrary to the wishes of "the people," and the result was an official recognition of cultural difference but an institutional denial of serious political status for groups seeking to establish political identities based on ethnicity or culture.[25] This, then, was the third influence working against the construction of an ethnic or cultural national identity in Russia.

Soviet nationality policies laid the groundwork for a federal structure that was the fourth significant factor leading to a Russian national identity centered on civic and economic concerns. At bottom, that structure was based on the division of the Soviet Union into territorial units designed to manage cultural diversity. In the first all-Union constitution of 1924, for example, national-territorial areas were designated for historical peoples that had never had them before. New boundaries also dissolved a number of preexisting territorial units, constructing new units that cut across old borders; and this "mixing of peoples" continued, especially under Stalin, just prior to and during the Second World War.[26]

As a direct result of these and related policies, Yeltsin found himself the president of a federation composed of territorial units divided into a hierarchy. The top of the hierarchy in 1993 consisted of twenty-one "ethnic republics" with their own (nominal) constitutions, flags, national anthems, and (real) tax privileges. Most of the remaining sixty-eight "Russian regions" were more unambiguously recognized as citizen-subjects of the federal center in Moscow.[27] However, the "ethnic" bases for these distinctions was rather suspect since in 1989 only five of Russia's then twenty republics had non-Russian ethnic majorities, while in some republics the percentage of Russians exceeded 90 percent.[28] Despite the fact that those officially recognized as ethnic Russians formed the majority of the population in most of the republics, tensions between the republics and regions were exacerbated by the fact that federal resources tended to flow away from the more productive "Russian" regions and into the less productive "ethnic" republics.[29]

These asymmetrical federal arrangements significantly influenced Yeltsin's discursive strategies, which shifted over time. Sometimes, like Lenin, he openly encouraged the increased autonomy of "nations" within the federation; at other times, like Stalin, he utterly shut down those aspirations when they threatened the integrity of the federation. In his struggle with Mikhail Gorbachev in the final years of the Soviet Union, Yeltsin openly supported increased autonomy for both the Soviet and Russian republics.[30] He encouraged what ultimately became a "parade of sovereignties" after outspokenly advocating the independence of the Baltic (Soviet) republics; and as late as August of 1990, he suggested to the other republics to "take as much freedom as you can swallow."[31] By the end of that year the Soviet republics, as well as the republics within the Russian Federation, had adopted declarations of sovereignty.[32] When the Russian regions (and even some cities) subsequently began to argue for their own local sovereignty and equal status with the republics, it remained to be seen if the Russian Federation could maintain its structural integrity.

Yeltsin's early strategy (encouraging political decentralization) was of limited value once the Russian Federation had achieved its independence, but his rhetorical alternatives were also limited. Articulating an overtly ethnic or cultural Russian identity was not a viable option, given the cultural variety within the federation, the historical impact of Marxist theories and Soviet policies, and the structure of the federation itself. Therefore, having moved from a position critical of federal power before his election to the presidency to a position representative of federal power after his election, Yeltsin's strategy shifted; and he then attempted to tame the centrifugal forces he had helped to unleash and reverse the separatist tide through constitutional reform.

### The Constitutional Battle in Post-Communist Russia

After Russia's Declaration of Independence in 1990, the need for a new constitution was undeniable. Russia was suddenly a new state, the collapse of the centralized economy and the Communist Party created an enormous political vacuum, and the old Brezhnev-era constitution based on Soviet assumptions and using Soviet terminology was now irrelevant for the new post-Communist reality. In the chaotic months after independence, the outdated constitution had devolved into "a cafeteria-style constitution in which contending politicians could choose sections and clauses to suit their political interests."[33] Problems were compounded by the fact that Russia had almost no experience with anything remotely like a balance or separation of powers, or a relatively healthy public sphere; for up until the final years of the Soviet Union, the state was not broken up into branches, and there were few opportunities for public argument. Instead, the legislative and judicial branches served merely as rubber stamps for Communist Party dictates. The civic dimensions of national identity were very weak indeed.

Given such a context, the redistribution of federal power and the establishment of a new constitution would be anything but easy for Yeltsin. The informal constitution of the Soviet Union had always been the body of Communist Party rules and norms, and Russia's constitutional history was anything but democratic.[34] Only the last czar, Nicholas II, begrudgingly accepted a constitution after statewide anarchy in 1905, but he discarded the constitution and dissolved successive parliaments shortly thereafter. Party leaders from Lenin to Brezhnev viewed prevailing constitutions as instruments to augment and legitimize Soviet power, not to limit or share it. Yeltsin, however, had been involved with constitutional reform issues throughout much of the Gorbachev era and was well positioned to begin the difficult task of constructing a new basic law that would reconsolidate the state by redefining center-periphery and interbranch relations.[35]

The drafting of a new constitution actually began in the late *perestroika* period, when Gorbachev still presided over the USSR and Boris Yeltsin had just begun his ascent in Russian politics. In 1989 the USSR Congress of People's Deputies had established a Constitutional Commission to draft a new all-Union constitution, but the quest was stillborn when the USSR officially collapsed in 1991. Following the partially competitive elections to the newly created Russian Republic Congress of People's Deputies, the Russian government established its own Constitutional Commission to codify Russia's sovereignty and define the new state structures. The Commission was chaired by Yeltsin and, not insignificantly, co-chaired by future archenemy and future Speaker of the Supreme Soviet, Ruslan Khasbulatov. Shortly thereafter, a smaller working group was established of some fifteen Supreme Soviet deputies and a roughly equal number of legal experts under the chairmanship of Oleg Rumyantsev.[36]

Rumyantsev and most of the working group were committed from the beginning to the "territorial principle," the belief that areas comprising the Russian Federation should enjoy equal legal status unrelated to ethnicity and/or culture. They were, in other words, committed to dismantling the republic/region dichotomy. They argued that a country as large and as culturally diverse as Russia would be incapable of sustaining democracy if administrative divisions reinforced ethnic consciousness.[37] From the outset, however, the symmetric federal ideal (based on the equality of territorial members) met with opposition from defenders of the asymmetric ethnic federalism of the Soviet era.[38] The symmetrical ideal is based on the assumption that equal representation tends to reduce center-periphery and inter-provincial conflict, but all early attempts to equalize representation and construct symmetrical federalism in Russia were stymied by the inability of regions and republics to agree to an equal legal status. Executive and legislative organs at all levels struggled to redefine state power as republics sought to maintain their privileged status. Simultaneously, the "crisis of dual authority" created by the collapse of the Soviet Union and the inadequacies of the Soviet constitution, with the executive branch struggling to seize a significant share of legislative authority and the legislative branch trying to seize a significant share of executive authority, led to a titanic (and arguably antidemocratic) struggle over the concentration of this "dual authority" into a single political will.

The core of the political struggles surrounding the construction of the new constitution focused around attempts on the part of various political players to emerge victorious out of the institutional and legal vacuum created by the collapse of the Soviet structure. In the absence of compromise, different political factions within Russia began to create competing drafts of the new constitution, with few seriously focused on the creation of a strong independent judiciary and all attempting to consolidate power for their own faction. By March of 1992, the Constitutional Commission's draft met with significant opposition from the creators of two alternative drafts, the first drawn up by a group of legal experts associated with Anatoly Sobchak, Mayor of St. Petersburg, and the second by Yeltsin's legal advisor, Sergey Shakhrai.[39] From that point on, "presidential" and "parliamentary" versions of the constitution began to take center stage as tensions between the executive and legislative branches continued to grow—tensions reflected in constitutional drafts threatening to subordinate one branch of government to the other.

By the early spring of 1993, Khasbulatov, now Speaker of the Congress and Chairman of the Supreme Soviet,[40] had increased his leverage over the drafting process and was actively promoting a "parliamentary" constitution that arguably represented the interests of local feudal elites from the old centralized economy who stood to lose the most through Yeltsin's policies.[41] Although Yeltsin remained technically the chairman of the Constitutional Commission, Shakhrai's draft "was more to his liking because it advocated a strong presidential republic, whereas Rumyantsev's gave more power to the Parliament."[42] Unable to reach a compromise, and given the mixed legacy of the executive branch's early market reforms, the legislature made moves in March of 1993 to reduce Yeltsin's powers, thus working to ensure that the parliamentary draft would be adopted. Angered by the continued deadlock over the new constitution, especially moves to reduce his decree-making power, and pressured to take a stronger executive stance by advisors, Yeltsin went on national television on 20 March, 1993, to announce a "special rule of government" in which all legislative authority would be subordinated to the executive branch.[43]

But what would Yeltsin's rhetorical strategy be? How would he characterize the national character? From the preceding review of nationalities policies and federal arrangements in Russia and how they influenced the constitutional debates, Yeltsin could certainly be expected to focus on the civic and economic dimension of national identity rather than ethnic or cultural dimensions, but how? Here, the observations of Russian scholar Michael Urban are particularly helpful, for he argues that the Soviet system led to a "broadly shared" and unique discursive code in the wake of the Soviet collapse.[44] According to Urban, "the repression of communication by the [Soviet] party-state prevented individual and collective identities from circulating in society" and therefore "no political identity was able to stabilize itself."[45] The Russian public was anything but accustomed to competing political parties, to the give and take of public discourses providing concrete policies, or to the reasoned public defense of those policies. Instead, they were accustomed to empty public discourse full of stock phrases with little or no meaning for them personally.[46] Given this general lack of faith in public discourse and the fact that the old system of government was generally blamed for the economic problems facing Russians in 1993, politicians attempted to dissociate themselves from the discredited past and their own responsibility for the old system, and instead attempted to project that discredited past onto their political opponents. As a result, politicians would consistently identify their political opponents with the label of "Communist," "Soviet," or "Bolshevik" and their own (vague) political programs with the will of "the people" and "democracy." Universally applied, it was this very strategy that naturally tended to outrage political opponents, since the leaders of both the executive and legislative branches used it. As we shall see, this "code" was certainly present in each of Yeltsin's addresses and in the responses to them.

Together, these observations about Russia's unique political history provide a context for better understanding national identity construction after the collapse of the Soviet Union. In addition, they suggest criteria for "successful" articulations of national character in the post-Communist era. Given the inherited federal arrangements and the risks of ethnic or cultural articulations of national identity, the general weakness of the public sphere, and the lack of compromise in the constitutional struggle, political actors in the post-Communist era could be expected to engage in the following strategy of remembrance: (1) to focus on the civic and economic dimensions of national identity, not on the ethnic or cultural dimensions; (2) to associate themselves with "democracy" and "reform," and their opponents with the "Soviets" or "Communists"; (3) to claim that only they are interested in the kind of compromise and balance and separation of powers required of functioning democracies (when in fact, few of the principal combatants were interested in compromise or balancing and separating powers, and instead most were intent on securing exclusive powers for themselves); and (4) to claim to be the true defenders of "the people" without providing detailed arguments about the form and logic of their policies. Unlike the situation in Germany, where both sides of the political debate sought to dissociate themselves from responsibility for National Socialism through two different and relatively complex rhetorical strategies, what made a speech "controversial" in 1993 Russia was when political actors representing the legislative and executive branches of government followed the *same* relatively basic strategy of remembrance. That strategy was clearly expressed in Yeltsin's controversial public discourse.

### Yeltsin's "Special Rule of Government" Speech

By early 1993 the battle lines had been drawn between a constitutional draft that would make the executive branch dominant and a draft that would make the legislative branch dominant; and given the considerable social upheaval caused by the economic "shock therapy" proposed by Western advisors, the office of the Russian president took a beating when the Eighth Congress of the People's Deputies convened on 10 March.[47] The Congress, in light of the early results of executive reforms, decided to strip Yeltsin of his temporary powers to issue decrees, appoint regional administrators, and guide legislation.[48] Recognizing the growing threat to his power and the potential shift of the balance of power to the legislative branch, Yeltsin felt compelled to respond, arguing in his memoirs that he

> was faced with a serious choice after the Eighth Congress. Either the President would become the nominal figurehead, and power would be transferred to the Parliament, or he would have to take some measures to destroy the existing imbalance of power. . . . There had been similar parliamentary rebellions in international practice, and it was no accident that Gorbachev had talked about presidential rule. The president either temporarily restricts parliament's rights or he dissolves it, and the Constitution once again begins to operate in full force after the elections.[49]

Choosing to "take measures" toward "presidential rule" and "destroy the existing imbalance of power" created by the "parliamentary rebellion," Yeltsin, with the help of a group of lawyers and speechwriters, drafted an "appeal to the people" that he delivered on 20 September in an attempt to outflank his opponents in the legislature.[50]

After a brief introduction in which he promises to "open [his] heart" and "share what has developed, decisions that have been made, how [he] is going to act, and the steps [he] plans to undertake," Yeltsin immediately makes the task of his leadership clear: in electing him president, "the people" had made a decision to no longer "keep sliding into the blind alley of Communism" but "to start comprehensive reforms, to embark upon the road of progress, the road of all civilized humanity."[51] Initially keeping the notion of "reform" vague, Yeltsin would ultimately explain that necessary, if painful *economic* reforms had already begun, according to the will of the people, but that "communists" in the legislature were jeopardizing those reforms. Accordingly, Yeltsin appealed to "the people" as follows:

> Thanks to you, esteemed compatriots, real transformations have begun in this country. Through our concerted efforts new forms of existence are striking root in Russia, but this is a slow and painful process. The country can no longer live under the circumstances of the ongoing crisis of power. Today, it is abundantly clear: all our problems are not rooted in the conflict between the executive and legislative branches of power, not in the conflict between the President and Congress. The essence is somewhere else; it is deeper. It is in the profound contradiction between the people and the former Bolshevist anti-people system which has not yet disintegrated, which today again seeks to regain its lost power over Russia. The Eighth Congress has, in fact, become a rehearsal for revenge of the former Communist Party *nomenklatura*.

Yeltsin continued, "The constant statements of loyalty to the Constitution are lies." "The constant references to the opinion of the voters and oaths of allegiance to democracy are lies."

Early in his speech, then, Yeltsin made a series of artful dissociations.[52] He argued that this was not a struggle between the executive and legislative branches of government (even though Yeltsin's main political opposition was to be found in the legislative branch) but between the fledgling "democracy" and the lingering "communist" menace. His political opponents were liars, deceiving the people when saying that they were democrats in support of a balanced constitution. The *true* democrats, the undeceived, within such a construction, become anyone not part of the "Bolshevik anti-people system." Having dissociated himself from the *"nomenklatura"* (despite the fact that Yeltsin was the Communist Party leader in the Sverdlovsk region in 1986 and rose to power within the ranks of the Party)[53] and having implicitly associated himself with "the people," Yeltsin went on to argue that "the communists" (in the legislature) were trying to regain unlimited power through an "anti-constitutional coup." He further maintained that "the separation of powers" was being "eliminated" and that the Constitutional Court was simply standing by and watching "the massacre against the foundations of the constitutional structure" that was purportedly taking place.

Despite his earlier claim that the conflict was not between the executive and legislative branches, Yeltsin next engaged in a direct attack on Khasbulatov, the Speaker of the Supreme Soviet, declaring that "the Speaker, in fact, [had] called for resuming the Cold War," and that due to his actions "the last hurdles on the road to the omnipotence of the Congress, the Soviets, and the Parliament [had] been removed." After blaming the Constitutional Court for contributing to this state of affairs ("the Constitutional Court has not as yet taken a position of principle"), Yeltsin concluded the first half of his speech by declaring that there were "as if two governments in Russia: one is constitutional, the other one abides in the Supreme Soviet."

By the mid-point of the March speech, then, Yeltsin had associated himself explicitly or implicitly with truth-telling, selflessness, the people, democracy, the civilized world, progressive economic reform, and constitutional government. Conversely, he had identified the leadership of the Supreme Soviet (but not the legislative branch!) with lying, selfishness, communism, the tyrannical and dictatorial past, the uncivilized world, economic backwardness, and unconstitutional government. The second half of his address built on these distinctions:

> I do not know whether the people's deputies understand this, but I am sure that it is well understood by the architects of the Eighth Congress: the functionaries of the former CPSU [Communist Party of the Soviet Union] Central Committee who have found a comfortable place in the Supreme Soviet and work there. At the Congress and at the Supreme Soviet, it is they who rule the roost. We must not allow the old Party *nomenklatura* to regain power in Russia. Russia will not survive another October Revolution.

Having now made a historical connection between the communist Supreme Soviet and the threat of another October (Bolshevik/Soviet) Revolution, Yeltsin announced that he had signed a "decree on the special order of governing the state until the crisis of power has been overcome."

Once Yeltsin announced his "special order," he made the connection between the communist menace and the legislative branch complete. He argued that because the "Congress declined to heed the voice of the country," and because the "Congress does not mean Russia," and because he was "authorized with the state responsibility to ensure the observance of the foundations of constitutional power," he had no choice but to enact measures that would thwart the Congress's attempt at a "constitutional coup." Yeltsin decreed that a statewide referendum would be held on 25 April in which he would ask for a vote of confidence, adding that "the people" would decide "who is to govern the country: the President and the Vice-President or the Congress of People's Deputies." Clearly it had to be one or the other.

For the moment, while not going so far as to dissolve the legislature, Yeltsin stated that "any decisions by any bodies or officials on the territory of Russia encroaching upon the foundations of constitutional power shall not be carried out." Of course, just which "foundations of constitutional power" Yeltsin was referring to (his "presidential" draft) is obscured by such discourse. What Yeltsin meant, but could not say, was that no one would be allowed to pass legislation limiting executive authority. Under the still-existing Brezhnev-era constitution, it was actually Yeltsin who was engaging in an anticonstitutional coup and encroaching on the foundations of constitutional power.

Having claimed that if "the political chaos" were not stopped and "resolute measures" were not taken, "the country [would] be plunged into anarchy," the speech then turned to a list of "priority economic measures" that would guide market reforms in the near term. His first economic priority was "to privatize land," the second was "to ensure that privatization will be irreversible," and the third was to provide "support for small and medium-sized businesses." The rest of the measures were designed to counteract the problems already created by "shock therapy": to organize social works, to combat inflation, to compensate "the tens of millions of people whose deposits in the savings banks have depreciated in the course of the reform," and to bring about "order in the granting of benefits and privileges to [large] enterprises," where there had been "too many abuses and instances of corruption." After enumerating that list, Yeltsin concluded his speech by claiming that what he was doing was "a civilized way out of the crisis based on fundamental constitutional principles" and that, because of his popular election, it was also "the choice of the people." Arguably, these latter rhetorical moves suggest that Yeltsin's ultimate concern was with the nature and pace of economic reform rather than with democratic political reform (particularly since he did *not* focus on institutional reforms that might have helped to guarantee a separation and balance of powers or legal reforms capable of reversing the "instances of corruption").

Yeltsin engaged in the posited strategy of remembrance by focusing on the civic and economic dimensions of national identity (the need for a democratic constitution and the continuation of market reforms); by associating himself, his vision of economic reform, and his constitutional vision with "democracy" and his opponents' with the "Soviets"; by claiming that only he was interested in an effective balancing and separation of powers; and by claiming to be the true defender of "the people" in the absence of reasoned arguments for carefully thought out policies.

As would be expected, given that this was the main rhetorical game in town, the response to Yeltsin's speech in Russia was swift, vehement, and similar. At 11:30 that evening, Vice-President Alexander Rutskoi, Deputy Chairman of the Supreme Soviet Yuri Voronin, and Chairman of the Constitutional Court Valery Zorkin issued a joint statement on statewide television announcing an emergency session of Congress to declare Yeltsin in violation of the constitution. Power was to be transferred to Rutskoi.[54] On the front page of the nationalist weekly *Den'*, Nikolay Pavlov argued that because of Yeltsin's unwillingness to acknowledge the "impoverishment of the population" caused by recent market reforms, he was compelled "to blow up a myth about the alleged conflict between the executive and legislative authorities."[55] The Eighth Congress, according to Pavlov, had simply attempted to return the balance of power to the constitutional norms prior to the granting of exceptional powers, whereas Yeltsin had become "a hostage of the West."[56]

The attacks on Yeltsin were widespread. In an open letter to Yeltsin in *Nezavisimaia Gazeta*, a paper widely recognized as an aggressively prodemocracy newspaper and voice of the Russian intelligentsia, the editor and chief Vitaly Tretyakov asked what the euphemisms "presidential rule" and "special rule of government" meant, and who had put the terms in his speech.[57] Tretyakov also wanted to know how the Russian Parliament could be conceptualized as "an enemy state," and why the president found it so difficult to struggle with the opposition as was done in functioning democracies. In the same issue, Valentin Tolstyh noted:

> The "evil" Council of People's Deputies supported Yeltsin's favorite idea about the sovereignty of Russia and started the dissolution of the USSR, elected him Chairman of the Supreme Soviet, and then supported his candidacy into the presidency. Therefore, when the position of the "communist" Council coincided with the position of Boris Yeltsin he not only tolerated but recognized and relied on it. Now that the Council has become a hindrance, an obstacle, he must eliminate it by any means possible. What is this if not an attempt to replace the torturously emerging democracy with autocracy?[58]

*Pravda*, the central organ of the parliamentary opposition, accentuated the "autocrat" theme. In the issue following Yeltsin's address, the front page displayed a cartoon of Yeltsin kicking the constitution out of the Kremlin and referred to Yeltsin as "Czar Boris." In the next issue, *Pravda* published a lengthy article in the form of a critical conversation with Yeltsin's speech. According to the writer, Yeltsin had plunged Russia into "wild capitalism." Referring to Yeltsin's dissociation between "the people" and "the communist Congress," the author argued that what was really happening was "a revolution from above," and that it was "not surprising that [Yeltsin's] team [was] carrying out its revolution under the disguise of demagogic phrases about love for the people."[59] Implicitly, such responses suggested that the parliament was in fact the defender of the people and the source of true democracy, while explicitly maintaining that Yeltsin and his supporters were liars using the discourse of democracy to mask undemocratic motives.

Yeltsin and his defenders, of course, characterized things quite differently. Yeltsin claimed he was surprised by the violent reaction to his appeal, especially from Vice-President Rutskoi, for all he was doing "was banning any decisions by Parliament that would limit the powers of the President of Russia."[60] Despite his surprise, Yeltsin stated that he was nevertheless pleased with the hostile reactions, for they helped to "reveal the line of political resistance" and proved to his satisfaction that Zorkin, Rutskoi, and the leadership of the Supreme Soviet had "declared war on the President."[61] In Washington, Clinton declared that "Yeltsin's challengers in Parliament [were] operating under a communist-era constitution" and that Yeltsin had shown "a great deal of courage in sticking up for democracy."[62] Strobe Talbott called Yeltsin "the personification of reform . . . the personification of post-Soviet life" but refused to characterize the parliamentary opposition.[63] An official statement by representatives of the executive branch of the Russian government appearing in the pro-Yeltsin newspaper *Izvestiya* supported the president's actions, arguing that they were "aimed at protecting citizens rights, liberties, and safety and at ensuring democratic conditions . . . and the preservation of the constitutional system as a whole," and continued to urge "all citizens of the multinational Russian Federation to show self-control, calm, and resoluteness in continuing Russia's democratic and economic transformations."[64]

In *Rossijskie Vestie*, the official organ of the executive branch, Andrey Kolesnikova observed that Yeltsin was simply responding to the parliament's attempts to limit his power and that "as a result of the [Congress's] constitutional coup d'état the President started a counter coup d'état."[65] Boris Grushin, a popular member of the President's Council, mirroring Yeltsin's characterizations, stated that "from the very beginning" there had been "an uncompromising conflict of old and new power represented on the one hand with pre-*perestroika* Bolshevik Soviets and on the other hand with embryonic presidential rule." As a result, according to Grushin,

> In the consciousness of our society, as well as abroad, there emerged a historical aberration. People defending the so-called Parliament, the so-called constitutional order, holding in their hands Brezhnev's constitution, got a chance to call themselves and to be perceived by others as supporters of constitutional rule. At the same time people fighting totalitarianism and attempting to weaken and eliminate soviet power and to put in its place a real democracy not only received the name but also started looking like usurpers of people's authority and autocrats and dictators.[66]

Clearly, Yeltsin's speech had triggered radically divergent characterizations, with both sides claiming that they were for "real democracy" and that their opponents were merely autocratic imposters.

In the months leading up to the adoption of the new constitution, as Robert Sharlet has noted, "the political and increasingly personal conflict over constitutional models became the driving and most divisive factor of Russian transitional politics."[67] This conflict, in turn, led to two completely different characterizations from two different camps using the same basic strategy, with both publicly claiming to be the true democrats. The dominant characterization of the pro-Yeltsin forces portrayed the Congress, in particular the Supreme Soviet, as being populated by former Soviet officials attempting to control the Russian government in order to reestablish power. Yeltsin, conversely, was portrayed (and portrayed himself) as a frustrated democratic reformer, blocked at each step by a recalcitrant and self-serving group of ex-Soviet officials ensconced in the other branches of government (especially the Supreme Soviet). According to Yeltsin, he had a right to do as he thought best because the people had declared their will by electing him president.[68] The Congress of People's Deputies was really not a congress at all, but a puppet of former communist officials attempting to drag Russia back into the past. All of the talk about democracy and reverence for the Soviet-era constitution coming from his opponents was nothing less than a cynical cover-up for their selfish desire to hold on to power at the expense of the future of the people.

Yeltsin's opponents offered a radically different characterization. For them, the temporary exceptional powers granted to Yeltsin had led to unbridled reforms that had impoverished large segments of the citizenry. What Yeltsin called democracy was nothing less than a brutal and irresponsible plunge into "wild capitalism," and his economic and political actions were actually destroying, rather than building, democracy in Russia. Members of both the legislative and judicial branches, as well as participants in the construction of early drafts of the constitution, consistently maintained that Yeltsin was using the discourse of democracy to disguise the imposition of an authoritarian presidency. It was they—the variously combative communists, nationalists, environmentalists, monarchists, agrarians, and so forth—who were the true democrats and the true representatives of the people. Yeltsin's efforts to construct a new constitution were primarily driven by a desire to control the state through rule by decree and to weaken the relative power of the legislative and judicial branches of government. They insisted that all of the talk about democracy and respect for the constitution coming from Yeltsin was a cover-up for the establishment of an undemocratic constitution.

### Yeltsin's Opening Address to the Constitutional Assembly

Yeltsin narrowly escaped being impeached for his March address, but he achieved his overall objective when, at a referendum on 25 April, to the great surprise of most observers, he received votes of confidence for both himself and his government's economic policies.[69] Having publicly unveiled his presidential version of the constitution on the eve of the referendum, Yeltsin interpreted the results as a vote of confidence for his vision of constitutional reform as well.[70]

The presidential draft envisaged the abolition of the Communist Party and the Supreme Soviet and their replacement by a bicameral legislature to be known as the Federal Assembly. The lower chamber (the Duma) would be popularly elected, but the upper chamber (the Federation Council) would be composed of appointed executive heads of regional administrations (appointed by the president) and elected leaders of the republics (thus ensuring tight presidential control over the upper chamber of parliament). As early as mid-October 1991, the Supreme Soviet attempted to pass laws ensuring that regional administrators would also be elected, but Yeltsin vetoed the legislation, thus allowing him to continue filling the posts.[71] No presidential appointment, save for the prime minister, needed to be approved by the parliament in Yeltsin's draft, and the president would have the right to dissolve the parliament and call for new Duma elections under specified conditions. The post of vice-president was to be abolished, only the upper house could ultimately impeach the president (which would be unlikely, given that a solid majority of the members would be hand picked by the president), and procedures for amending the constitution would be made more difficult.[72]

Yeltsin's preferred draft was presented to the Constitutional Commission on 6 May, 1993, and was rejected the very next day when the newest iteration of the parliamentary version of the constitution was unveiled. In the parliamentary draft, which radically opposed Yeltsin's, the president was to become merely the ceremonial head of state instead of the leader of a broadly empowered executive branch. Bolstered by the vote of confidence received in the April referendum, Yeltsin decided that the best course of action was to convene a Constitutional Assembly to accelerate the constitutional process.[73] Continuing to be encouraged by repeated calls from advisors to construct a "strong presidency," Yeltsin opened the Assembly on 5 June with a speech designed to justify limiting discussion to his presidential draft and to embellish his characterization of the distinctions between "democratic Russia" and "the Soviet model of power."[74]

The Assembly, attended by some seven hundred government officials, trade unionists, representatives of political parties, and parliament deputies, had been hand picked by Yeltsin's staff. They also controlled the Assembly's agenda to ensure that the final agreement on the draft constitution would be based on the model of a presidential republic.[75] The diverse composition of the group and the gravity of the situation, however, also ensured that the convention would have its controversies. Outside of the Assembly there were organized demonstrations by defenders of the legislative branch, with estimates ranging between five and ten thousand protesters.[76] More dramatic still were the confrontations on the floor of the Assembly. After Yeltsin's provocative address, Khasbulatov attempted to intrude on the schedule to respond but was jeered off the stage. He then stormed out of the proceedings along with some fifty fellow delegates, and communist deputy Yuri Slobodkin was forcibly removed by guards after demanding to present the Communist Party's draft of the new constitution.[77]

Yeltsin's address, which took more than forty minutes to deliver, continued to develop the strategy of remembrance offered in March by embellishing his monumental history of "democratic Russia" and establishing in even more plain terms how the "Soviets and democracy" were "not compatible." The speech, divided roughly into four sections, was a lengthy account of Yeltsin's repeated attempts to construct a "true democracy" based on sound constitutional principles (which he described in great detail) in the face of reactionary communist opposition. The first section was a lesson on the "democratic traditions" in Russian history and how the Bolshevik revolution was an interruption of Russia's democratic evolution.[78] The second section offered an indictment of the Soviet system of government and the outdated Brezhnev-era constitution inherited by the Russian Federation, linking the legislative branch of government to the Bolshevik seizure of power. Section three provided a beautiful picture of a "genuinely democratic Russia" and explained the importance of the existing, albeit temporary, Federation Treaty. The Treaty, signed three months earlier in March, was an attempt to define the relative powers of the federal center and the periphery, and it significantly enhanced the rights and authority of the subjects of the federation.[79] The final section stressed the importance in a democratic society of a balance of power between the various branches of government and concluded by suggesting a procedure for the adoption of the new constitution (based on a "strong executive").

After formal introductions, Yeltsin began his speech by proclaiming that with "the adoption of a constitution, the creation of a genuinely democratic republic in Russia will be complete."[80] Maintaining that democracy had been interrupted by the October Revolution, which had "proclaimed a republic of Soviets," Yeltsin argued that a "new republic was being born" based on "private property, the Federation Treaty, presidential power, constitutional supervision, and a multi-party system" (63). Weaving "presidential power" (instead of a balance and separation of powers) into the assumptions of the new republic, Yeltsin then traced a history of "democratic" traditions in Russia, claiming that Russia "contributed . . . to the world's treasure chest of democracy." Pointing to the reigns of enlightened autocrats such as Peter the Great and Alexander II, the opening section of his speech concluded that the current constitutional crisis was impeding the inevitable return to the path of democracy and that if "a democratic and lawful statehood" were to be established in Russia, then the "arbitrary rule of the [Soviet] authorities" would have to stop.

After reasserting the dichotomy between the "democratic traditions in Russia" (of which he and the people were a part) and the antidemocratic traditions of the Soviets (the deceptive opponents of the people), Yeltsin launched into an extended attack on the "the Soviet model of power." As the speech progressed, Yeltsin rhetorically painted two contrasting scenarios that echoed the strategy of remembrance articulated in his March address. The first was a vision of a democratic Russia thriving under the guiding force of his suggested constitution, while the second was a disturbing portrait of the remnants of Soviet power imposing arbitrary rule and stifling democratic reform. Yeltsin started his attack by stating that "the judiciary can be turned into a reliable repository of constitutionality, law, and order only if we make a phased withdrawal from the Soviet model of power" (64). The people of Russia, according to Yeltsin, were suffering under the yoke of the much-amended Soviet constitution and the Soviet system of government. "Soviet constitutions restrained nothing and protected nobody," Yeltsin warned, but "were tools of the Communist Party to legitimate their arbitrary wielding of power" (64).

Continuing his attack on the "Soviets," Yeltsin argued that the most recent communist tool for arbitrarily wielding power was the Brezhnev-era constitution, for it did "not guarantee the unity of the country or a stable, peaceful, and secure life for its citizens" (64). Instead, the constitution left Russia with the system of Soviets that were inherently antidemocratic. Returning to his history lesson, Yeltsin reasoned that because "the Soviets disbanded the Constitutional Assembly which had emerged after democratic elections in 1918," the "present representative bodies . . . remain the successors of power . . . seized by force. They are not legitimate as far as a democratic system is concerned" (66). Yeltsin emphasized that the Soviets had never managed to overcome their authoritarian roots, despite the trend toward democratic reform in the late 1980s and 1990s, and that "the representative power inherited . . . from the Soviet system is unable to reach the accord we need so much today" (thus implying his own desire for compromise). The Soviets, according to Yeltsin, were based on "the force of lawlessness . . . [and] the Soviet form of power was not capable of being reformed." Therefore, he declared, the "Soviets and democracy are not compatible" (63). It was this phrase that formed the heart of Yeltsin's strategy, and it was also the phrase that triggered the broadest range of negative reactions in the Russian media. By portraying the constitutional crisis as the result of a systemic flaw, he effectively traced the problems facing the country to the Bolshevik regime and, by association, to the system of Soviets (the institutional apparatus of the Communist Party), which in turn was associated with the legislative branch of government (where Yeltsin's political opponents were located).

In contrast to his characterization of the "dysfunctional, anti-democratic Soviet constitution" and the "the crisis of power" at the time, Yeltsin next offered an extended vision of a "genuinely democratic republic" of Russia based on the principles of "human rights, entrepreneurship, stability, federalism, and a balance of powers" (63). He maintained that "extensive self-government," "a division of powers," "the Federation Treaty," and "the effective combination of a presidential republic with parliamentarism and an independent judicial power" alone could ensure Russia's continued democratic growth. "For the first time in the history of Russia," Yeltsin concluded, "no one institution of the state will have the opportunity to monopolize power." The task was not "trying to score a victory over one another, but finding accord" (again masking the extraordinary executive powers in his draft, while simultaneously assuming the role of the compromiser) (69–70).

Despite such democratic claims, Yeltsin and his supporters still insisted that a "strong authority" was needed to accomplish these democratic goals, and they characterized efforts at establishing a presidential republic as the only reasonable way to establish a "true democracy." Sergey Alekssev, one of many controversial individuals responsible for publishing the presidential draft of the constitution, argued that

> Yeltsin's proposed constitution expressed [the drafters'] hopes of establishing a strong, well-functioning, and self-confident authority, and this is the first principle of our constitution. The second component of Yeltsin's proposed constitution, also expressed in the deputies' demands, is to provide a true democracy for every single person. And the essence of the concept behind the constitution, with which I hope it is hard to argue, consists of the fact that a strong, reliable, and stable authority must exist in a democratic regime.[81]

A "true democracy" in Russia, in other words, required a strong leader, capable of implementing unpopular but "needed" political and economic reforms and unimpeded by a recalcitrant opposition.

Yeltsin's speech precisely built on the strategy of remembrance in the March address. He focused on the civic and economic dimensions of national identity while reinforcing his image, through a variety of discursive moves, as a democrat fighting for the future of the Russian people against communists who were trying to use the legislative branch as a means to destroy not only the presidency but democracy itself. Yeltsin developed his earlier association of "the Soviets" with the October Revolution when he characterized Russia as having always had democratic tendencies. The democratic impulse in Russia had been interrupted by "the Soviets," leading to seventy years of oppressive Bolshevik rule, and another antidemocratic revolution was at hand. Yeltsin once again associated the term "Soviets" with the former communist *nomenklatura*, which in turn was associated with the "representative powers." Finally, arguing that the Soviets were inherently antidemocratic and were wielding arbitrary power by hiding behind the old constitution and refusing to compromise, Yeltsin concluded that the Soviets (his political opposition) and democracy (Yeltsin and the executive branch) were not compatible.

Not surprisingly, reactions to the speech by defenders of the legislative branch were less than positive. Furthermore, they once again revealed how Yeltsin's political opponents also claimed to be "democrats" fighting for "the people" while accusing "Czar Yeltsin" of desiring a return to the past. Despite Yeltsin's explicit call for a constitutional democracy based on a balance of powers, Khasbulatov accused Yeltsin of having "Czarist pretensions" and described the Assembly as "the illegal start of a dictatorship" and an "attack on democratization and on democratic institutions."[82] Mirroring statements made in March, the parliament's radio station broadcast that Yeltsin's democratic aspirations were a "myth."[83] Continuing to characterize Yeltsin as a would-be dictator, a headline in *Rossiskaia Gazeta* proclaimed that "Representational Power Will Exit and Dictatorship Will Arrive."[84] And a headline in *Pravda* declared that "Democracy Is Under the President's Thumb," warning of a "dictatorship crawling impudently and cynically, trying to gain a foothold," and claiming that the Assembly was the "conclusion of the anti-government revolution started on the 20th of March." [85]

In the same article in *Pravda*, Zorkin, Rumyantsev, and Slobodkin were each highly critical of Yeltsin's remarks. Zorkin argued that "we came here in the hope that we would find a place for national accord, that this would be a council—a round table—which Russia needs so much. We saw something completely different." "I think the people of Russia," added Zorkin, "will sort this through and understand who supports justice and who wants to impose dictatorship." Slobodkin, the delegate who had been forcibly removed from the proceedings, stated that he had not expected Yeltsin to attack the entire legislative system so savagely. "From the very beginning of the Constitutional Assembly there were offensive remarks about the Supreme Soviet, the [Congress] of the People's Deputies, the system of [local] Soviets, and other organs of representative authority. I could hardly wait until the speech was over because it was so contentious. I do not support Khasbulatov, but I felt personally offended."[86] Rumyantsev, among the deputies who left the Assembly after Yeltsin's speech, made a list of conditions that would have to be satisfied before the offended parties would return. Foremost of those concerns was that there be "addresses by the Supreme Soviet and the Constitutional Commission in addition to Yeltsin and his supporters" and that all parties have a voice in the proceedings.[87]

Other critiques included a front-page editorial in the same issue of *Pravda* (June 8) entitled "Address to the Citizens of the Russian Federation," signed by fifty "leaders of the Russian Federation." According to the editorial,

> The President of the Russian Federation, Boris Yeltsin, gave a speech at the Constitutional Assembly on 5 June 1993, in which he did not conceal direct threats and offenses to the Congress of People's Deputies, the Soviets, and all organs of the people's rule. All aspects of the situation in our country, including the situation in the Constitutional Assembly, show that a dictatorship of one person with unlimited rights is being reborn in our long-suffering Russia. Democracy, for which our people struggled with so much pain, is now under threat.[88]

Finally, Victor Trushkov argued that "Yeltsin's act of depriving the legislative branch of the right to speak," his "utter neglect of the judicial and legislative authorities," and his "monarchical constitution" were all proof of the "pseudo-democrats . . . being unable to accept the very principle of constitutionality."[89]

Defenders of the legislative branch, also following the dominant strategy of remembrance, argued that Yeltsin was attempting to institute a dictatorship and that all of his talk about democracy was a smoke screen for an insidious attempt to destroy what little democracy there was in Russia. Yeltsin was a "pseudo-democrat," and his democratic aspirations were a "myth." Conversely, the true democrats, the true defenders of "the people," were the members of the legislative and judicial branches advocating the parliament's constitutional draft.

By the end of the Constitutional Assembly, therefore, the discursive battle lines were even more clearly drawn. While the defenders of both the presidential and parliamentary drafts publicly claimed to be the "true" democrats (and accused their opponents of being "false" democrats), neither of the dominant drafts proposed a serious balance of powers. Yeltsin's draft attempted to subordinate the legislative and judicial branches to the executive branch, while the parliament's draft attempted to subordinate the executive and judicial branches to the legislative branch. Yeltsin wanted to retain the right to rule by decree, appoint regional executive authorities, and obtain the right to dissolve the parliament; while the parliament wanted to reduce the president to a figurehead. Both groups focused on the civic and economic dimensions of the Russian crisis, both associated themselves with democracy and their opponents with the authoritarian past, both claimed to be the only ones seriously interested in compromise, and both claimed to be the sole defenders of the people (without providing reasoned arguments in support of concrete policies). It was this "democratic" battle that continued to rage throughout the summer as the criminal takeover of Russia's natural and financial wealth continued apace.

### Yeltsin's "Constitutional Coup"

Given the dramatic conflict on the opening day of the Constitutional Assembly, Yeltsin quickly worked for a compromise.[90] Eventually a draft was hammered out and approved by the Assembly on 12 July, 1993, without Khasbulatov's participation, and was promptly sent out to the provincial authorities for comments. Most local legislatures and executives, however, either rejected the draft or attached unacceptable amendments. Leaders in both the republics and the regions, capitalizing on the weakness of the center created by the "crisis of dual authority," continued to demand more and more power, using the discussion over the new constitution to voice various demands. As a result, the Constitutional Assembly failed to construct a politically viable draft.

By late summer the combatants had become desperate, unable as they were to create a draft of the constitution based on the principle of shared and balanced power. It was increasingly evident to Yeltsin and his advisors that the conflict with parliament was effectively blocking an outcome favorable to a "strong presidency." Therefore, in early August, Yeltsin openly threatened the parliament with dissolution if they continued to refuse to work with him (i.e., to adopt his version of the constitution).[91] On 18 September Khasbulatov publicly complained that Yeltsin should be removed from office because he was nothing more than a "common drunkard" attempting to impose a "dictatorial, plutocratic regime" and warned that any attempt to dissolve the parliament would immediately lead to his impeachment.[92] In the meantime, the Supreme Soviet began to draw up a package of constitutional amendments that would accomplish the goals of the parliamentary draft and finally reduce the president to a figurehead.[93] In light of this impending event, Yeltsin carried out his threat; and on 21 September, declaring that Russia was "experiencing a profound crisis of its state structure," he issued Decree 1400 "On the Step by Step Constitutional Reform of the Russian Federation."[94] The decree dissolved the existing parliament, announced the creation of a new form of parliament consistent with Yeltsin's preferred constitutional arrangements, and requested the temporary suspension of the activities of the Constitutional Court.

Here Yeltsin's discursive strategy took root in concrete political action. After declaring that the "difficult reforms" could not be pursued or "elementary order" maintained because of the crisis of state structure, Yeltsin stated that he had "to stop the dangerous developments and to put an end to the abuse of the rule of the people." Referring to the April referendum, Yeltsin argued, "The Supreme Soviet's majority is openly trampling the will of the Russian people. They pursue a course toward weakening and eventually removing the President and disorganizing the work of the present government. A strong propaganda campaign aimed at discrediting totally the entire executive branch has been unleashed in Russia." Noting a number of decisions recently passed by the parliament related to presidential powers and the economy that contradicted "the interests of the people," Yeltsin averred that "while the legislators [kept] pledging fidelity to the constitution and the laws . . . constitutional reform ha[d] been virtually halted."

Yeltsin then launched into an extended attack, initially not on the entire legislature, but specifically on the "leadership of the Supreme Soviet." He accused them of blocking "the constitutional process without giving any coherent reasons," of "deliberately undermining the legal basis of the young Russian state," and of writing a "drastic revision of the existing constitution" in order to engage in the "evil practice of taking arbitrary legal actions." According to Yeltsin, "that kind of law has nothing in common with legality, especially when it is dictated by one person or group of persons." Obliquely referring to Khasbulatov, Rutskoi, Zorkin, and others who resisted his presidential draft, Yeltsin argued that "all power in the Supreme Soviet of Russia has been seized by a group of individuals who have turned it into the headquarters of a die-hard opposition" and that "the only way to overcome the paralysis of state government in the Russian Federation [is] to fundamentally renovate it on the basis of the rule of the people and constitutionality."

The very accusations that had been leveled at Yeltsin were now reflected back onto Khasbulatov and his closest supporters. From the perspective of the opposition, it had been Yeltsin all along who was engaged in a propaganda campaign against the legislative branch, working to associate the (relatively) democratically elected assembly with the old (thoroughly undemocratic) Soviet system. It was Yeltsin's ability to appoint cabinet ministers and local executive authorities without oversight that most closely resembled the ethos of the old Soviet system. Khasbulatov and other defenders of the parliamentary draft had argued that Yeltsin and a handful of close advisors were plunging Russia into a desperate economic situation and that a dictatorship was coming. Yeltsin, however, began his address by arguing just the opposite: these were in fact the characteristics of Khasbulatov and his "group."

Having made these accusations, Yeltsin then announced he had "issued a decree endorsing amendments and alterations in the current constitution of the Russian Federation." He announced the suspension of the Congress of People's Deputies and the Supreme Soviet and the construction of a new Federal Assembly based on the model he had proposed just prior to the April referendum. Maintaining that he did "not seek any personal gains" by the move, Yeltsin voiced his hope that the new parliament would not be populated by "people who engage in political games at the expense of the people" but by people who were "more competent, more cultured, and more democratic." Reiterating that the Congress should not attempt to convene, Yeltsin concluded by saying that the measures he had taken were "the only way to protect democracy and freedom in Russia, [and] to defend reforms of Russia's as-yet weak market" and calling upon the "good sense and civic awareness" of the people in support of his move.

The reaction to Yeltsin's speech is well known. In a more serious iteration of the March events, Khasbulatov gave a hastily prepared press conference after

Yeltsin's address and called upon the people to "rise to the defense of democracy" and "the people's elected representatives."[95] At the same press conference, Zorkin announced that the Constitutional Court was about to begin an emergency session to discuss the constitutionality of Yeltsin's actions. After midnight the Supreme Soviet met, adopting a resolution "On Terminating the Powers of Russian Federation President B. N. Yeltsin." Rutskoi took the oath of office as president and immediately declared Yeltsin's decree invalid.[96] As the crisis mounted in the following days, Yeltsin, in another of his "democratic" moves, banned the publication of several papers opposed to his decree and censored front-page articles in moderate papers as well.[97] When the Constitutional Court quickly determined that Yeltsin had exceeded his constitutional authority and could be impeached, he issued a decree suspending their deliberations.[98] For two weeks, armed supporters of the parliament occupied the parliament building. After attempts to take over the state-run television station led to bloodshed, Yeltsin, after several tense hours, convinced the military to attack. In the end, more than 125 people were killed, more than 600 wounded, and more than 100 of the "rebels" were in prison, including Rutskoi and Khasbulatov.[99]

By now the basic strategy of remembrance had become commonplace. Yeltsin's supporters told the usual story. The headline of *Rossijskie Vestie* proclaimed, "The President of the Russian Federation Boris Yeltsin, Elected by the People of Russia, Addressed All the Citizens of Russia in a Critical Moment for Our Country to Give Their Voice to Democracy." In the United States, the story was the same. The *Washington Post* reported that Yeltsin had crushed the "rebellion" in order "to stamp out the vestiges of communism and complete the transition to a free-market economy."[100] In Russia, the authors of editorials supportive of Yeltsin openly admitted that his actions constituted a "coup d'état" but argued that there really was no choice, given the political conditions in the country.[101]

For Yeltsin's opponents, those actions were concrete proof of his dictatorial intentions, now acted upon. Since opposition presses (and some editorials in moderate presses) were censored after Yeltsin's decrees, it is difficult to assess the precise ways in which the situation would have been publicly characterized. However, according to Fred Kaplan, a reporter for the *Boston Globe*, one censored article described the scene in the Kremlin after anti-Yeltsin demonstrators broke through police barricades surrounding the parliament building, and other censored articles urged Yeltsin to reverse the decree and negotiate with parliament.[102] By this point, however, Yeltsin's characterizations had led to concrete actions, the "coup" had succeeded, and only time would tell what the new Russian "democracy" would look like.

## Post-Coup Developments and the New Russian Constitution

Having removed the "obstructionist" parliamentarians from the positions of power, thus preventing them from hindering his own vision, Yeltsin's first step seemed a logical one. He decided to reconvene a Constitutional Assembly in November to finally reach agreement on a draft of the new constitution. However—and perhaps unexpectedly for some—Yeltsin did not seize the opportunity to open dialogue with others, and the Assembly produced a "strong presidential draft." After the events in early October, Yeltsin and his staff made no attempts whatsoever to consult Assembly delegates or regional leaders about major constitutional changes. As a result, many provisions concerning the balance of powers between branches of government and between the center and periphery were weakened or removed to the advantage of the executive branch.[103]

While the constitution that emerged after Yeltsin's "democratic coup" may have been a shock to many Western observers, it should not have been. Despite the inordinate amount of praise for Yeltsin's democratic pretensions and the popular distinction in the U.S. press between the "communist" parliament and the "democratic" executives, considerable evidence accumulated between 1991 and 1993 suggesting Yeltsin's "autocratic" tendencies.[104] As James Hughes has noted, there was "an over-simplistic assumption that the primary political dynamics of the [Russian] conflict ha[d] involved 'democratizing' forces at the center" and "an 'old regime' coalition of resistance to reform" in the parliament.[105] It is surely a fact that the legislative branch was populated by many ex-Soviet functionaries more concerned with maintaining and building their own bases of power than with building a society based on the rule of law, but the picture was much more complicated. According to Hughes, the conflict between the executive and legislative branches of government "should be understood less in terms of an 'ideological' schism [between] 'democrats' and 'communists' and more accurately as one of fracture and interplay over economic distributive and re-distributive issues between the two key strata of the old communist *nomenklatura*, the top layer in Moscow and the main sub-layers at the regional level, each battling to preserve and protect their status and extend their control over the country's wealth."[106]

Erik Hoffman also points out that Yeltsin "periodically demonstrated an instrumental attitude toward constitutions and constitutional law" and "never seems to have understood that the national legislature and judiciary can enhance the efficacy and legitimacy of constitutional law."[107] As early as 1991, Dimitri Simes pointed out that the new Russian political class surrounding Yeltsin were mostly "products of the old totalitarian establishment" and that Russian parliamentarians with the strongest democratic credentials lost access to Yeltsin after his election to the presidency.[108] Edward Walker also noted that in the months following Yeltsin's election he "moved quickly to strengthen his presidential powers at the expense . . . of the legislature, and local governments."[109]

From the very beginning of his presidency, Yeltsin was denounced by his opponents as an authoritarian sacrificing liberals and surrounding himself with representatives of the *nomenklatura*. After his March address, a compromise had been reached with Khasbulatov in which the referendum could only proceed if Yeltsin would replace his innovative, market-oriented prime minister, Yegor Gaidar. Tellingly, Viktor Chernomyrdin, well known for his corrupt ties with the emergent industrial oligarchs, turned out to be the eventual alternative.[110] By early 1994 serious reforms had ground to a halt as the executive branch divided into a "political government" run by Yeltsin and an "economic government" run by Chernomyrdin.[111] Scholars almost universally now recognize that the kind of state created by Yeltsin is at best a "delegative democracy,"[112] a "return to the Russian system of the Tsars,"[113] or an "authoritarian democracy."[114] Whichever term is applied, each one refers to a weakening of the legislative and judicial branches and a strengthening of the executive branch, especially the president.

### Possible Functions of the Discourse of Democracy in Russia

Who were the *true* democrats during Russia's transition? After all, what *is* a *true* democracy? Those rare instances in history when some relatively large percentage of (usually male) citizens participated in public debate on issues of state directly affecting them look little like the governments of any modern state. Direct democracy, it would appear, has all but disappeared. Even direct democracy's usual replacement, representative democracy, may be a dying breed. Cambridge political theorist John Dunn goes so far as to say that "what democracy is is a highly desirable label for which the exceedingly heterogeneous class of modern states show a strong predilection when they come to describe themselves in public."[115] There are no *true* democracies; there are only different state leaders calling their widely heterogeneous governments democracies. Perhaps this is what is *true*. In Russia, we have seen everyone call themselves the *true* democrats, but what were the political consequences of their characterizations?

According to the democratic theory of Ernesto Laclau and Chantal Mouffe, political battles, which are ultimately material/institutional battles, are fought with the weapons of words.[116] It is not that there is or is not a true democrat, instead there are various "democratic" discourses meaning radically different things and having radically different institutional consequences. *True* democracy is procedural, is a practice: it is an incessant and plural critique of consensus and identity itself. There are, then, more or less "democratic" discourses, if by the term we mean discourses that question authority, balance and separate powers, institutionally multiply sites of critique, and direct the attention of citizens to socially unjust policies.[117] Instead of asking "who is the *true* democrat?" perhaps the more appropriate question to ask is "who benefits by, and who pays because of, different 'democratic' discourses?"

How did the discourses of democracy ultimately function in Russia? In light of the constitution eventually adopted by the Russian people in 1993, and given the subsequent weakness of the Russian state,[118] it appears that a great opportunity was missed because the tenuous balance of powers actually beginning to take root was prematurely pulled. Yeltsin and the executive branch were basically assuming the role of neo-liberal capitalists, and the legislative branch was basically assuming the role of neo-Soviet socialists. Both roles, however, had more to do with securing economic and political power than with developing a healthy market democracy. Had the legal foundations been present to encourage the development of these two "parties," had Yeltsin been willing to have regional representatives elected, had Khasbulatov not been attempting to also undermine a balance of powers, had the privatization process been handled in a less corrupt manner, and had advice on viable constitutional reform been more effective, a "truer" democracy may have had a chance.[119] The political players, however, were mostly former Soviet elites unable to recognize that democracy means incessant struggle and compromise and that the so-called crisis of dual power was in fact the violent and contentious emergence of a fledgling democracy. Neither the legislative nor the executive branch was particularly democratic (although the legislative branch slowly developed a relatively democratic process despite the eventual constitutional imbalances), and neither enjoyed familiarity with the kind of power critique required in healthy democracies. Therefore, a logical question to ask is why the U.S. government was so eager to proclaim Yeltsin a democrat and to encourage the dissolution of the opposition.

As early as March 1993, the U.S. government publicly supported Yeltsin's attempt to force through a new constitution based on a strong executive, with State Department officials arguing that "if Yeltsin decided that the only way to move forward with political and economic reform was to dissolve the Parliament and rule temporarily by decree, the United States would be sympathetic."[120]

After the "rebellion" in October, Strobe Talbott argued that the attack on the Russian parliament building had actually been handled quite delicately, adding, "We have stressed what we feel is a self-evident fact—that for international financial support, whether from the private sector or international financial institutions, money will not be well-spent and will not improve the lot of the Russian people, unless fundamental economic reforms are in place and under-way."[121] Talbott rejected accusations from congressional leaders such as Senate Minority Leader Bob Dole that "the United States might have contributed to the crisis by putting pressure on Yeltsin to make unpopular economic reforms."[122] Also ignored in the implementation of "fundamental economic reforms" required by "international financial institutions" was the widespread criminali-zation of the economy precipitated by those reforms.[123]

It appears that economic reform, much more than political reform, was at the heart of Russia's "democratic" transition. As Kaplan remarked in the days following the attack on the parliament building, Yeltsin's constitutional coup meant that the "policy of moving from socialism to capitalism" had emerged victorious over "the step back to a more state-managed economy, as favored by the majority in Parliament."[124] The unfortunate connections between Yeltsin's attempted pace of reform and international economic pressures has become increasingly clear in recent years, and as Richard Sakwa notes, "The Yeltsin presidency was marked by the consolidation of [economic] liberalism but not of democracy."[125]

Regardless of motives, it is a fact that the dominant strategy of remembrance in 1993 Russia (and in the United States) was that Yeltsin and the other demo-crats had to dissolve the communist parliament in order to establish democracy. Russian national identity was publicly imagined to be a struggle over civic and economic policies guided by a democratic constitution. However, while Russia is certainly more democratic today than it was under the Soviet system, the "free markets and democracy" strategy disguised the criminal economic takeover of the natural and financial resources of the state. Between 1991 and 1998, while Russia's gross domestic product dropped by 55 percent and industrial produc-tion dropped by 75 percent, the newly emergent, often self-proclaimed busi-ness "oligarchs" gained increasing influence over the state. The best way to take advantage of "reforms" during the Soviet collapse was to buy commodities such as metals and oil at low, state-controlled prices in Russia and then sell them abroad at world prices. Serious-minded reformers in early 1992 tried to end this "rampant embezzlement" by freeing Russia's commodity prices and exports, but the state energy lobby, led by Chernomyrdin (who became minister of energy that May and soon after prime minister), "resisted ferociously."[126] Nevertheless, this "free markets and democracy" strategy was successful enough to resonate with two presidents of the United States, the U.S. State Department, leaders of the Russian military (who came to the defense of Yeltsin), close constitutional advisors, and the Russian people (who failed to rebel against Yeltsin's move). The question is, why was this strategy so successful, particularly given the terrible economic hardships average Russians had to endure?

One possible and suggestive answer has been provided by William E. Scheuerman, who argues that the erosion of representative democracy over the last several decades has been accompanied by the expansion of the "exceptional powers" of executives within quasi-democratic societies. It is a "natural" consequence of globalization that the inefficiency of deliberative government must be replaced by an economically savvy class of executives capable of making economic and political decisions on behalf of the (uninformed) people. According to Scheuerman, "elected popular legislatures . . . have undergone an often dramatic erosion of political influence in [the 20th] century," and "administrative agencies now exercise significant law-making functions."[127] The reason for this shift from deliberative democracy to authoritarian democracy (which is by no means complete or unavoidable) is that the granting of exceptional executive authority is an instrument of "effective" economic management.

David Lempert has made an argument similar to Scheuerman's, maintaining that "the future of the former Soviet Union in the New World Order is as part of a network of international corporate structures in a parallel to feudalism" (rather than as part of a growing network of healthy democracies).[128] That is, the post-Soviet states (and elsewhere), including Russia, while using the discourse of democracy, are in fact constructing state structures that function to ensure an economic system that benefits those with access to capital and hurts the vast majority of citizens. Lempert maintains that "the transition in Russia does not bear any of the marks of a citizen-based democracy backed by the relatively equal distribution of property and resources that would allow for checks on concentrations of economic, political, or military power," but instead it shows marks of having succumbed to a "larger and more unassailable world system."[129]

Ultimately, given the general lack of democratic traditions in Russia, given the old Soviet constitution's weaknesses, and given the ugly fistfight that the debate over the new constitution became, it is too easy to simply blame Yeltsin. All indications suggest that he truly believed he was fighting to establish "free markets" and to save "democracy." There is also the fact of the unfortunate relationship between Yeltsin's Russian advisors, Western advisors, and pressures from what Talbott referred to as "international financial institutions," and how their advice was translated into constitutional reform.

It is also difficult to assess the specific forces that are causing so many of the multicultural federations around the globe to break apart into nation states. Yeltsin and his appointed successor Putin have succeeded in keeping the Russian Federation together, but given the fact that the Russians have received very little advice from political scientists about the intricacies of democratic engineering, it is becoming increasingly clear that Yeltsin's presidential constitution will likely not be "strong" enough to hold back the centrifugal tendencies of our globalizing world or to help in any meaningful way to decriminalize the Russian economy.

# CHAPTER FOUR

# Shifting Strategies of
# Remembrance in Quebec

In the closing years of the twentieth century, the logic of the nation-state was working its magic not only in Europe and Eurasia but on the North American continent as well. In Canada, on 30 October, 1995, citizens of the province of Quebec voted for the second time in fifteen years to declare their independence, and for the second time they voted to remain Canadian. But it was a very close call. Unlike a similar referendum in 1980 where the No vote won by almost twenty percent, in 1995 the No vote carried by just over one percent.[1]

Having had yet another opportunity for establishing a new state slip between their fingers, *Québécois* nationalists were devastated and exhausted. A few burned Canadian flags, a crowd of Yes supporters surrounded the No headquarters in Montreal, and the riding office of liberal leader Daniel Johnson was burned to the ground.[2] Staunch secessionists expressed continuing anger at anglophone and allophone minorities in the province, whom they believed ruined the Yes side's chances in the referendum, and the voting statistics indicated that their belief was not unjustified.[3]

The results of the referendum revealed that *Québécois* separatists had failed to articulate a national identity appealing enough to persuade a sufficient number of non-francophone citizens of Quebec to vote for secession. Yet on the evening of the referendum's narrow defeat, such a fact apparently could not be acknowledged publicly by one of the central leaders of the secessionist movement. Appearing on national television, Quebec Premier Jacques Parizeau rose to address Yes supporters, stating that sovereignty had been lost due to "money" and "the ethnic vote." Although newspapers across Canada and Quebec before, during, and after the referendum reported that Parizeau's statement was factually true, public reactions were so universally and strongly negative that within days, like Jenninger in West Germany, he was forced to resign his office.

Why was one of the principal architects of *Québécois* secession forced to resign for stating facts that were openly acknowledged in newspapers across Canada? What might be the relationship between the dramatic rejection of Parizeau's speech and the somewhat puzzling desire on the part of many French Canadians to secede from Canada? Indeed, it is a puzzle to many that Canada, one of the world's most prosperous and peaceful federal states, has been wracked in recent decades by continued attempts on the part of provincial leaders in Quebec to secede. Nevertheless, an active secessionist movement has been going on for more than a quarter-century in Quebec. Why?

One clue was offered in a 1995 scholarly conference on the relationship between globalization and the exercise of state power, where organizers discussed a central paradox of our times: while borders are becoming increasingly irrelevant with the rise of mass communication technology and transportation systems, larger political units are fragmenting, states are trying to incorporate citizens, and numerous smaller nation-states are emerging.[4] As theorists of nationalism consistently point out, the process of modernization has led to people's increased mobility, which in turn has undermined traditional forms of local cultural identification. As individuals find themselves increasingly uprooted from traditional and more "readable" forms of community, the task of *creating* identities has increasingly fallen on the state.[5] This process of "nation building" was going strong at the end of the twentieth century not only in Germany and in the new states created by the collapse of the Soviet Union but also in Quebec. Perhaps, then, the desire for an independent Quebec nation is partially a result of globalization, the loss of tradition, and the consequent fabrication of strong feelings of national belonging by the state.

To isolate the dominant strategies of remembrance during the 1995 Quebec referendum, an analysis of the public discourse of state representatives in the months immediately before and after the 1995 referendum, with particular emphasis on Parizeau's dramatically rejected speech and the responses to it, once again proves a fruitful approach for analyzing the public articulation of national identity. "The study of ethnicity and nationality," Paul Brass notes, "is in large part the study of politically induced cultural change. More precisely, it is the study of the process by which elites and counter-elites within groups select aspects of the group's culture, attach new value and meaning to them, and use them as symbols to mobilize the group, to defend its interests, and to compete with other groups."[6]

We have already seen this process at work in West Germany and Russia, where state leaders sought to erase fascism through the discourse of "victimage" and to associate "democracy" with economic, political, and legal reforms that ultimately compromised the development of a "democratic marketplace." Cornel West argues that, ultimately, collective identity is less about "democracy" and more about managing "the distribution of resources."[7] Immanuel Wallerstein concurs when he states, "The fundamental role of the state . . . as an institution in the capitalist world economy is to augment the advantage of some against others in the market—that is, to reduce the 'freedom' of the market. . . .

[T]he state is a special kind of organization. Its 'sovereignty' . . . is the claim to the monopolization (regulation) of the legitimate use of force within its boundaries, and it is in a relatively strong position to interfere effectively with the flow of factors of production."[8] Could this be a motive for nation building in Quebec? Could it be related to globalization? And what might "money" and the "ethnic vote" have to do with it?

## Two Visions of Canada

Anyone seeking to understand recent national identity construction in Canada must first come to terms with the history of cultural, political, and economic conflicts between the English and the French in Quebec. Like Russia, and unlike Germany, Canada is a multicultural federation. However, whereas Russia is truly *multi*cultural, Canada's federation is principally *bi*cultural, with a large concentration of French-speaking citizens in Quebec. The First Nations, or the descendants of the peoples living in Canada before either the French or English arrived, constitute a third smaller, yet politically important cultural group. The Russian Federation has dozens of "hot spots" where identity entrepreneurship could erupt at any time, given the right political and/or economic conditions. In Canada, Quebec is the hot spot.

The fundamentally bicultural nature of Canada causes citizens of Quebec to be simultaneously interpellated as belonging to two imagined communities: the provincial and the federal.[9] Citizens of Quebec, therefore, are oftentimes torn between two allegiances: one for Canada and one for Quebec. Most English-speaking Canadians believe (and are encouraged to believe) that Quebec is an integral part of an indivisible country composed of one nation: Canada. Conversely, many citizens of Quebec believe (and are encouraged to believe) that they are a conquered and colonized people and that the only way to overcome their minority status within English Canada is to obtain their own country through secession. Such an "identity dilemma" can lead to social unrest, as Will Kymlicka has pointed out, for "if citizenship is membership in a political community, then in creating overlapping communities [e.g., federal and provincial], self-government rights necessarily give rise to a sort of dual citizenship, and to potential conflicts about which political community citizens identify with most deeply."[10] This tension between allegiances can lead to what Gregory Jusdanis refers to as "culture wars," or the *use* of culture as a means for mobilizing publics for the purposes of the state.[11]

Over the course of two hundred years, but particularly since the 1960s, these two competing visions (of a predominantly English pan-Canadian identity and of a predominantly French-Canadien identity situated in Quebec) have been institutionalized through language legislation, initiatives on the part of educational and cultural ministries, and constitutional reform. Together, these practices and initiatives have served to strengthen *Québécois* identity in unique ways by building upon perceived historical injustices and consequently constructing a politically useful collective identity.

### The Historical Basis for Contemporary Québécois Nationalism

Quebec's official motto, on every motor-vehicle license plate in the province, is *"Je me souviens"* (I remember)—but who exactly is this "I," and what exactly do the citizens of Quebec remember? Many historians, journalists, and political theorists agree that key memories helping to define the present relationship between the French and English in Canada can be traced to the so-called Conquest of 1763, a military event that marked the beginning of tensions that persist to this day.[12] Christian Dufour argues that "Canada is profoundly dependent on the conquest of 1763" since "Quebeckers are still very much affected by the aftermath of the . . . conquest they experienced in the 18th century, which remains buried in their collective unconscious."[13]

Between 1608 and 1759 a French Colony, New France, was settled on the banks of the Saint Lawrence River; but on 12 September, 1759, English soldiers clashed with French and New French soldiers on the Plains of Abraham, with the English emerging victorious. France subsequently decided New France was too expensive to maintain, and the English victory signaled the eventual colonial "subjugation" of the French in North America.[14] French Canadians, therefore, were both conquered by the British and simultaneously abandoned by their "mother country." What followed was a series of colonial measures explicitly designed to accustom the French Canadians to notions of British citizenship, establishing the foundation for more than two centuries of cultural and political conflict.[15]

As a result of the American Revolution, the population in Canada was transformed from a predominantly French society into a broader Canadian community where a swelling British population enjoyed colonial power at the expense of the French. For the next half-century, the predominantly Catholic French pursued farming and minor crafts, while the Protestant English minority became increasingly urban and secular. Economic and cultural divisions became more pronounced at the beginning of the nineteenth century, when the British thwarted the fledgling middle-class francophones in their efforts to achieve and maintain social status, and French Canadian nationalism began to take on a double nature. On the one hand, there was a conservative clerical nationalism that supported cooperation between the Catholic Church and the colonial English Canadians; and on the other hand, there were separatist nationalists, primarily members of the frustrated middle class, who argued that cultural and political survival could only be guaranteed in an independent French Canada (a theme to be repeated in the late twentieth century).

Rebellions in 1837–38, instigated by French Canadians eager to gain better political leverage, were prompted in no small part by the fact that the British minority were benefiting from their links with England at the expense of equal opportunities for positions of wealth and power.[16] To make matters worse, some of the British elite predictably had no patience for the ethnic nationalist aspirations of rebellious French Canadians. Britain's Lord Durham, sent to control the situation, perhaps best summarized the British attitude toward the French citizens of Canada when he stated: "I entertain no doubt of the national character that must be given to Lower Canada; it must be that of the British Empire. . . . I should indeed be surprised if the more reflecting part of the French Canadians entertain at present any hope of continuing to preserve their nationality. Much as they struggle against it, it is obvious that the process of assimilation to English habits is already commencing. The English language is gaining ground, as the language of the rich and of the employers of labour naturally will."[17]

The colonial period of French Canada between 1763 and the mid-nineteenth century, then, saw the suppression of political/economic separatist nationalism and the consolidation of French Canadian identity in the cultural/religious sector. The conservative clerical nationalism that emerged from the failed rebellions allowed the English to maintain their dominant positions in politics and the economy, while French Canadian identity became imaginatively centered on antimaterial and messianic sentiments. However, with the dawn of industrialization and urbanization in Canada toward the end of the nineteenth century, conservative clerical French Canadian identity began to lose its appeal. In 1871 Quebec was 77 percent rural, but by 1911 it was half-urban, and between 1900 and 1930 there was continued massive migration by the rural French Canadians to the cities.[18] These demographic shifts served to intensify the exposure of French Canadians to business environments dominated by the English, which in turn resulted in increased recognition of English economic hegemony. Renewed hostility on the part of a frustrated but growing French Canadian middle class, coupled with the values of conservative clerical ideology, combined to maintain the conception of a distinct French Canadian identity threatened by English hegemony even as the previously rural, Catholic, and poor French Canadians were becoming increasingly secularized.

The economic depression of the 1930s, followed by an expanded federal and provincial welfare state, along with the accumulated frustrations of more than a century of economic inequality furthered by clerical nationalism, eventually led to a sharp break in Quebec's political and social history. This dramatic shift in political orientation is commonly referred to as the "Quiet Revolution," or the gradual replacement of the authority of the Catholic Church with the authority of the state and the gradual modernization of francophone Quebec. Dufour nicely summarizes the change in ideological climate: "The energy that French Canada of the pre-Quiet Revolution years invested in religious activities, and the spiritual mission adopted after 1840 to compensate for the fact that true power had escaped it, were transformed around 1960 into a political nationalism, based on the use of the powers of the Government of Quebec."[19] The intellectual elite came to believe that they had been misled by the "old myths" and that English values and institutions were perhaps more appropriate for modern society than their own.

By the 1960s French Canadians were starting to shed the conservative clerical values and traditions that had previously defined their imagined community, taking on instead a more "English" (secular and urban) character. Simultaneously, the Quebec government began actively promoting "*Québécois* culture" by significantly expanding government departments of education and culture.[20] These moves, combined with a series of constitutional struggles, set the stage for an articulation of ethnic nationalist *Québécois* identity with almost enough collective appeal to motivate the majority of citizens of Quebec to secede from Canada.

As in Russia, the economic and civic dimensions of national identity played a significant role in exacerbating federal tensions and triggering the identity war between Quebec and the central federal government.[21] It was the ethnic dimension, however, that ultimately took center stage. By analyzing each of these dimensions (economic, civic/legal, and ethnic) in turn, a sufficient context will emerge for the analysis of Parizeau's dramatically rejected speech, the public response to it, and the strategies of remembrance at work during the 1995 referendum.

### The Economic Dimensions of Québécois National Identity

There is little question that most French Canadians, especially before the Quiet Revolution, were at an economic disadvantage when compared with their British compatriots. As more and more of the descendants of the New French, previously under the sway of conservative clerical nationalism, moved to urban areas, they increasingly became aware of the fact that English Canadians were basically in control of the economy. Justifiably angered and frustrated at the economic remnants of British colonialism, leaders of the subordinated group decided that the time had come to transfer cultural production from the Catholic Church to the provincial state.

The economic undercurrent of Quebec separatism is observed when one looks at the backgrounds of the two principal leaders of the *Parti Québécois* in 1995: Jacques Parizeau and Lucien Bouchard. Parizeau received his doctorate from the London School of Economics in 1955 and was an economic and financial advisor to the prime minister of Quebec from 1961 to 1969. Between 1976 and 1984 he held the following posts: president of the Treasury Board, minister of revenue, minister of financial institutions, and chairman of the Ministerial Economic Development Committee.[22] Bouchard, on the other hand, received his law degree in 1964 and worked in the 1970s in the areas of labor relations and collective bargaining. He has sat on the boards of the General Society of Quebec Finance (*Société générale de financement du Québec*) and the Canada Development Investment Corporation. On the political front, Parizeau was elected president of the *Parti Québécois* in 1988, and was leader of the official opposition in the Quebec National Assembly through 1994, when he was elected premier of Quebec on 26 September. Bouchard was elected to parliament in 1988 and in 1993 became leader of the official opposition in Ottawa. Thus, both men began their careers in the economic sectors of government and only later went into public office, eventually becoming leaders of the opposition on both the provincial and federal levels.

But the surest sign of the economic basis for Quebec secession is found in the public speeches by Bouchard and Parizeau in the months leading up to the 1995 referendum. Particularly revealing addresses include a speech Bouchard delivered at the opening session of the National Convention of the *Bloc Québécois* on 7 April, 1995, and speeches delivered by Parizeau on 7 October, 1995, for the inauguration of the National Yes Committee and on 17 October, 1995, before the student body at the University of Montreal.[23] Their rhetoric suggests that the primary function of the construction of a sovereign Quebec state was not only to protect the cultural heritage of the descendants of the inhabitants of New France but also to take economic control of the state for the advantage of the rising French Canadian middle and upper-middle classes. The speeches given by Bouchard and Parizeau in the months leading up to the referendum, therefore, were dominated by economic and cultural/ethnic concerns. The economic claims did not prove particularly controversial inside Quebec, but the cultural/ethnic claims did.[24]

Bouchard delivered a speech at the opening session of the National Convention of the *Bloc Québécois* in April of 1995 that exemplifies the centrality of the economy in the secessionist agenda. After beginning his address by noting that the *Québécois* "are a people . . . in a land where our ancestors settled almost four hundred years ago" (thus confirming the fundamentally ethnic character of the *Québécois* identity), he devoted almost half of the address to the creation of a "common Quebec-Canada economic space." Drawing on the model of the European Union, Bouchard argued that "Americans . . . [and] responsible Europeans are discovering that the new challenges of our day, whether they relate to economic stagnation and the growing inequalities it entails, or to the new international competitiveness, require . . . an even greater solidarity within the national communities." After discussing the implications of the North America Free Trade Agreement (NAFTA), concerns over the value of the Canadian dollar, and the "centralizing appetite of the federal state," Bouchard concluded by arguing that "the young people . . . [will be] the first victims of an economic slowdown," but that if "one has . . . a language and a culture of [one's] own . . . [one has] all that is needed . . . to exploit [one's] potential to the full."

Here, Bouchard explicitly argues that in order to "exploit" the contemporary economic situation (created by neo-liberal "free trade" policies), the nation's ethno-cultural identity must be strengthened. Nevertheless, true to Etienne Balibar's thesis on the fundamental incompatibility between ethnic nationalism and multicultural community building,[25] Bouchard qualifies his statement:

> The Quebec that we want to build is a Quebec for all Quebeckers. We must also see to it that cultural diversity is preserved in that society. But all of that must be in accordance with a fundamental priority; that priority is to integrate and combine all the components in our society in order to make a nation . . . a predominantly francophone unity. . . . [T]he nationalism of the *Bloc Québécois* . . . is an open and welcoming formula, respectful of differences, enriching itself from cultural diversity, rather than fearing or fighting it.

Bouchard ultimately argues that economic empowerment is most possible through the creation of a French-speaking nation, regardless of its ethnic make-up, but this argument is made after clearly articulating "the people" as the descendants of New France.

The confused relationship between economic nationalism, ethnic nationalism, and multiculturalism was simplified in Parizeau's public speeches, where the "diversity" issue was all but absent. In his address for the inauguration of the National Yes Committee on 7 October, 1995, Parizeau was ultimately concerned with preventing Montreal from becoming an "anglophone city." In his speech to the student body of the University of Montreal later that month, he was also concerned with persuading his audience that their economic future depended on a Yes vote in the upcoming referendum.

In his address to the Yes Committee, Parizeau argued that "[with] a Yes vote, we will immediately be able to create 25,000 jobs in research and development simply because we will have put an end to the federal injustice that appropriates our tax dollars and gives us less than our fair share." He then followed up with a long list of the ways in which the "No Clan" had consistently stood in the way of Quebec's economic empowerment. Enumerating more than a dozen examples, he ended the list with a lengthy discussion of how the "No Clan" fought against language legislation as well. Parizeau completed his speech by reinforcing a main theme of his address: a No vote would mean "accepting that Montreal will no longer be a largely francophone city within twenty-five years." Parizeau's address, then, focused on two related themes: the preservation of the French language, especially in Montreal, and local economic empowerment.

In his address to the students of Montreal, Parizeau also focused on the economy. After opening with remarks about how "the labor market is less than receptive," he asserted that the referendum constituted a "new beginning" and that a sovereign Quebec would belong to the students. He then launched into a lengthy discussion of the many economic benefits that would accrue from secession: specifically, it would mean jobs.

However, even though the focus of pre-referendum speeches by both Bouchard and Parizeau listed the many financial benefits that would supposedly accrue from secession, the ultimate economic impact of Quebec independence remained strikingly unclear.[26] Just two days before the referendum vote, Canadian Prime Minister Jean Chrétien painted a bleak picture of the economic consequences of secession in a public plea to the citizens of Quebec, arguing that whereas Bouchard painted a rosy picture, maintaining that a Yes vote would lead to a friendly economic partnership between equals, a Yes vote was a very dangerous gamble. Such a divergence in characterizations is perhaps not surprising, but given the significant economic impact secession might have had, it is an interesting fact that there was no serious public debate between federalists and separatists over the economic causes or consequences of secession. Instead, these economic considerations continued to be trans-muted into civic and ethnic considerations. This was nothing new, since con-cerns about language law and constitutional reform, coupled with concerns about protecting the culture of the New French, each had a long history in mobilizing French Canadians.

## The Civic Dimensions of Québécois National Identity

It is significant that, at the very point in history when French Canadians were taking on secular English political and economic values, the production of a *Québécois* identity was actively taken up by the state, particularly after the elec-tion of the *Parti Québécois* in November of 1976.[27] In the years following the Quiet Revolution, Quebec lawmakers focused primarily on the areas of lan-guage legislation and constitutional reform.

The relationship between language policy and identity in Quebec is a long one. Battles over language primacy have been waged since the Conquest of 1763, and the fear of linguistic and cultural assimilation has remained pro-nounced since the days of Lord Durham.[28] Control over language is deemed consonant with control over government, and the relationship is obviously a strong one. For Quebec separatists, one of the more recent and dastardly actions on the part of "English Canada" (the federal government) was former Canadian Prime Minister Pierre Trudeau's Official Languages Act of 1969. That Act brought a bilingual vision of Canada under the rule of federal law, infuriating Quebec separatists who believed it was specifically designed to dilute the "distinct society" status of Quebec.

William Coleman details the way in which Quebec's leaders responded to this federal language law, noting that the *Charte de la lange française* was the first major piece of legislation to be introduced by the *Parti Québécois* after its election to power. Introduced by the Minister of State for Cultural Develop-ment in April of 1977 and eventually known as Bill 101, the law mandated that all Quebec municipalities, school boards, and local health and social service institutions draw up all official texts in French only. In direct opposition to fed-eral law, according to Coleman, "Bill 101 left no barriers standing in the pub-lic sector to the creation of an integrated nation-state."[29]

As a response to the federal law creating pan-Canadian bilingualism, the *Parti Québécois* law appeared to anticipate the later advice of Dufour, who argued that francophones should "impose their mother tongue." According to Dufour, "For as long as the Quebec identity does not appropriate what was then [during the colonial period] the English strength [linguistic, hence economic and political hegemony], for as long as it does not become its own conqueror, it will be condemned, unfortunately, to lose the same battle . . . over and over again. This is a tremendous challenge: to stabilize the Quebec identity in relation to the Canadian identity. It is the psychological equivalence of independence, the conquest of the Conquest."[30] Here the colonial period is drawn upon as a justification for contemporary language legislation in the active promotion of cultural production and makes a good example of how imagined community is promoted by state policy. What Defour leaves unstated, however, is how Quebec's privileged constitutional position (discussed in the following pages) allowed its exclusionary language law to stand, despite federal law, thus making the "colonial" argument less than compelling. Nevertheless, legal control over the use of language in the province was crucial for the nation-building process, and it continued to play an important role, as witnessed in the remarks by Parizeau and Bouchard in the weeks leading up to the referendum on the importance of having a francophone state.

In addition to the legal skirmishes over language laws, the constitutional battles waged in Canada in the years leading to the two referendums were also related to the various strategies of remembrance employed at the time: (1) the federalists articulating a pan-Canadian bilingual and multicultural identity; and (2) Quebec separatists articulating a *Québécois* identity based on the French language and New French ancestry. On the one side of constitutional battles were federalists, such as Trudeau, who sought to defeat Quebec nationalism through the inclusion of a Charter of [Individual] Rights in a patriated Canadian constitution and the construction of a multicultural, bilingual, and pan-Canadian national identity. On the other side, Quebec nationalists sought to maximize provincial economic and political power through the constitutional recognition of the "two founding nations" thesis and the "distinct society" status of Quebec.[31]

For many, the principal impetus for the 1995 referendum on Quebec sovereignty was the patriation of the Canadian constitution (formally transferring the constitution from English to Canadian control) in 1982, a move that was itself a federal response to the 1980 referendum crisis. Trudeau maintained that previous Canadian prime ministers had failed in their attempts at patriating the constitution because any amending formula had to be unanimously approved by all of the provinces, "permitting every province to hold the country to ransom."[32] According to Trudeau, by September of 1980, in his own attempt to patriate the constitution by unanimous consent,

> It had become obvious that the greed of the provinces was a bottomless pit, and that the price to be paid to the provinces for their consent to patriation with some

kind of entrenched Charter [of individual rights that would supercede community rights] . . . was nothing less than acceptance by the federal government of the "compact" theory, which would transform Canada from a very decentralized, yet balanced federation, into some kind of loose confederation. That is when our government said, "Enough. We are going to give the people their Constitution and their Charter of Rights."[33]

A similar situation had faced the Soviet Union just before the collapse of the empire, particularly in 1990 and 1991 when republics, regions, and cities were declaring independence. When Yeltsin was attempting to construct the new Russian constitution, political leaders in the republics and regions played the same game of doing everything they could to maximize their local powers. To counteract the centrifugal tendencies exacerbated by that game in Canada, Trudeau hoped to create a form of constitutional (civic) patriotism designed to "create values and beliefs that not only united all Canadians in feeling that they were one nation, but also set them above the governments of the provinces and the federal government itself."[34] Therefore, in light of the "bottomless pit" of regional objections, Trudeau decided to patriate the constitution without the consent of the Quebec provincial assembly and in effect engage in his own "constitutional coup."

Separatists saw the patriated constitution as a direct assault on Quebec's "distinct" status. In a manner remarkably similar to the way leaders of the relatively privileged republics in Russia failed to work with Rumyantsev to create a federation of equals, LaForest argued that the new constitution treated unequals equally. Quebec was not equal to all the other provinces; it was equal to all of them put together. Trudeau defended his decision to patriate the constitution without Quebec's support because, in his opinion, the Quebec government would never have agreed on the proposed constitutional reforms, especially since the failure of reform could have been called upon as further impetus for secession. Trudeau furthermore argued that the provinces gained considerable power from the Constitution Act of 1982 in areas such as resource management, indirect taxation, and external trade. Most important, the provinces also obtained the right to opt out of certain federal laws, especially those affecting culture, through a "notwithstanding clause."[35] This constitutional clause had allowed the new French language laws to stand despite constitutionally mandated federal bilingualism. Trudeau's actions were nevertheless interpreted as treason by secessionists, who redoubled their efforts at attaining independence from the federation.

Although federalists believed that the constitution was considerably weakened by Quebec's refusal to approve it and by the inclusion of the "notwithstanding clause," on 17 April, 1982, Queen Elizabeth II gave her approval for the new Canadian constitution. This turn of events was a serious blow to the Quebec separatists, for England had officially transferred constitutional power directly to the Canadian people and diluted the force of claims of English oppression. But for separatists, according to LaForest, the Act merely invited the *Québécois* "to commune at the altar of a Canadian national spirit whose genealogy goes back to an English-Canadian nationalism."[36] It was clear to separatists like LaForest that the fundamental objective of the Charter of Rights and Freedoms woven into the constitution was to promote throughout Canada a political culture capable of reinforcing in each citizen the feeling of belonging to a single Canadian nation.

The patriation eventually led to other constitutional battles, but the primary significance of these battles for our purposes is the way in which they reflected separate rhetorical strategies related to the construction of imagined national community. The federalists, between 1980 and 1995, sought to construct a pan-Canadian identity based on individual rights, bilingualism, and multiculturalism; while secessionists sought to construct a *Québécois* identity based on communitarianism, monolingualism, and French Canadian ancestry.[37] These fundamental differences in imagined national identity led, in turn, to different strategies of remembrance in the years between the referendums. Prominent Quebec separatists, prior to the 1995 referendum, primarily sought to build national identity on the basis of the protection of ethnic culture, and the culture to be protected was French Canadian. Public articulations of *Québécois* identity drew heavily on traces of colonial memories of "conquest" and "abandonment" and frequently contained ethnic references.

After the Quiet Revolution, certain attributes of the French Canadian identity were transformed as the terms *Catholic, antimaterial,* and *rural* receded into the background, and the French language, French Canadian ancestry, and the "colonized" aspects of *Québécois* identity (with its attendant ethnic roots) came to the foreground. As a result, the strategies of remembrance of early *Parti Québécois* members were oftentimes based on the notion that a "true *Québécois*" (*pure laine*) would be a descendant of the settlers of New France, French-speaking, and free from English (federal/colonial) authority of any kind. The colonial history of the New French was totally submerged, only to erupt in later demands from members of the First Nations seeking to secede from Quebec should Quebec secede from Canada. The result of such a conception was the construction of a potentially xenophobic ethnic nationalist sense of imagined community inappropriate for a multicultural federation, but most effective for uniting a linguistically homogenous nation-state.[38] Federalists, conversely, sought to build a national identity based on individual rights and on the production of a pan-Canadian identity where bilingualism and multicultural-ism would prevail and could, as a side benefit, dilute the potential threat of French power in Quebec.

Regardless of the various potential strengths and weaknesses of federal and *Québécois* strategies, Quebec separatists often drew upon the image of the col-onized French Canadian to justify their secessionist agenda in 1995. Though provincial leaders in Quebec already possessed considerable constitutional con-trol over most economic, educational, linguistic, and cultural policies, they still sought to secede. The conservative clerical ideology of the colonial period con-tributed to English economic and political hegemony, and the articulation of a Quebec nation as "French Canadian culture under attack" had definite merit prior to, and in the early years of, the Quiet Revolution. Such an articulation provided provincial leaders with a powerful tool for recreating provincial/federal political relationships while simultaneously consolidating a national imaginary. But now that those relationships had been significantly transformed and arguments of "colonial" domination were increasingly suspect, the ques-tion that remained was how articulations of "national" character needed to change in light of the new economic and political realities. Here we begin to find the controversial addresses of Bouchard and Parizeau around the time of the referendum particularly instructive.

### The Ethnic Dimensions of Québécois National Identity

As the history of conflict between the French and English in Canada and the more recent maneuvers in language and constitutional law suggest, political and economic inequality in Canada has predominantly been transmuted into a cultural war over imagined (and institutionalized) national community. In this continuing struggle, the 1995 referendum constitutes the most recent major battle—a battle where skirmishes over ethnic issues provided the imme-diate context for Quebec Premier Jacques Parizeau's dramatically rejected address. Paradoxically, it was ethnic nationalist strategies of remembrance that ultimately provided the key impetus, as well as the key stumbling block, for the establishment of a *Québécois* nation.

Despite the long history of economic and political struggles between the French and English in Canada, almost every newspaper article appearing in the Canadian presses concerning the 1995 referendum was focused on ethnic issues. Furthermore, many of the pre-referendum statements by Bouchard and Parizeau revealed traces of ethnic nationalism.[39] To articulate a sufficient cultural/ethnic/racial difference, nation builders frequently draw upon a pos-tulated common heritage. Unfortunately for ethnic-nationalists, as noted by

Balibar and Wallerstein, such a postulated common heritage "run[s] directly counter to the nationalist objective, which is not to re-create an elitism, but to found a populism; not to cast suspicion upon the historical and social heterogeneity of the 'people,' but to exhibit its essential unity."[40]

Contemporary *Québécois* nationalism is no exception to this rule. Not only did Quebec's Declaration of Sovereignty state that the common heritage of the *Québécois* people is French Canadian, but the notions of "conquest" and "colonization" used in many secessionist arguments directly refer to the French Canadian past. This strategy of articulating common heritage as a justification for secession created considerable problems in 1995.

Just weeks before the referendum, Asselin Charles noted that "belonging in Quebec requires not the subscription to a set of values, or the demonstration of a number of qualities, but rather a certain '*Québécitude*,' the exclusive essence of those whose French ancestors settled in that part of North America."[41] Charles also noted that a label frequently used by nationalists for identifying "true Quebeckers" before the 1995 referendum, *pure laine*, literally means "pure wool," and referred to "old stock" *Québécois*, or the descendants of the inhabitants of New France.

The charges made by Charles about the ethnic nationalist basis of *Québécois* nationalism were echoed by others after Lucien Bouchard, generally acknowledged as the leader of the separatist movement in 1995, publicly complained just weeks before the referendum that white women in Quebec were not having enough babies.[42] In a speech delivered on 13 October, Bouchard stated, "Do you think it makes sense that we have so few children in Quebec? We are one of the white races that has the least children, [and] that doesn't make sense."[43] Rather than apologizing for the remark, both Bouchard and Parizeau argued that there was nothing wrong with the use of the phrase "white races." Parizeau flatly stated, "How do you want to call it? The pale race? I don't know. What's the deal? I don't understand. I don't see what's shocking unless you're nitpicking." Bouchard went on to argue that the No side was trying to make a mountain out of a molehill, arguing that it was "ridiculous" to consider him a racist.[44]

Despite Bouchard's and Parizeau's attempts to defend the "white race" remark, there was a painful if vague awareness that the ethnic dimension of *Québécois* identity was becoming increasingly problematic. Tu Thanh Ha observed that, contrary to the evidence supplied by most of the arguments for secession forwarded by LaForest, Dufour, and Parizeau, the more politically sophisticated "sovereigntists ha[d] soldiered on for years, trying to dispel the image of their cause as one born mainly to address the nationalist aspirations of the descendants of New France settlers."[45] As support for the claim, Ha pointed out that, in the spring of 1994, when separatist member of parliament Philippe Pare publicly complained that ethnic voters could deprive "old-stock Que-beckers" of independence, Pare was demoted from a key referendum planning committee by Bouchard, primarily because Bouchard had been attempting to make the term "*Québécois*" more inclusive. Additionally, in the first week of October, while campaigning in Val D'Or, when a radio host interviewing Bouchard used the word *Quebecker* in a way that implied "francophone Que-becker," Bouchard quickly corrected him.[46] Such "corrections" on the part of Bouchard suggest that he was well aware of the exclusionary meanings attached to the term *Québécois* and therefore sought to make his "white race" remark seem an aberration.

In the weeks leading up to the referendum, there was considerable contro-versy over the content of the terms "*Québécois*" and "Quebecker." On the one hand, Toronto journalists such as Charles and Ha were quick to point out the fundamentally neo-racist and ethnic nationalist character of the separatist movement. On the other hand, Bouchard, despite his "white races" remark, was struggling to make the term appear to be more inclusive; for as Charles noted, "The more lucid among the nationalist elites know that minorities and immigrants are an asset to the province. They must send them a more inclu-sionary message."[47] Nonetheless, in an anonymous editorial in the *Globe and Mail* on 17 October, 1995, entitled "Mr. Bouchard's Ethnic Nationalism," the writer argued that, although s/he believed neither Bouchard nor Parizeau were racists, "If Mr. Bouchard and Mr. Parizeau occasionally talk this way, it is because their movement, whatever its fervent denials, is rooted in ethnic, rather than civic nationalism. Blood is more important than citizenship. While they claim to embrace a wider world, the independentists advance an essentially insecure vision. Their language and culture may be safer than ever before, but they are unable to admit it because it would expose the emptiness of their cause." The writer also noted that "there has been a long strain of racial intol-erance among militant nationalists. Invariably it becomes a question of 'we or them.' Today, more precisely, it is a question of *Oui* or them."[48] This comment would prove prophetic, especially for Parizeau, in the weeks to come.

### Shifting Strategies of Remembrance in Quebec Nationalism

On the evening of the referendum's narrow defeat, the problematic conflict between the ethnic nationalist strategy of remembrance (providing a difference sufficient to justify secession) and a more inclusive strategy of remembrance (providing a similarity sufficient to draw non-francophones into the secession-ist camp) came to a head. Parizeau appeared before a large crowd of Yes sup-porters who had been on an emotional roller coaster throughout the day. His remarks were aired live by the Canadian Broadcasting Corporation (CBC) in French, with an English translation provided. Before addressing the crowd, Parizeau had spoken briefly with Bouchard by telephone, and Bouchard attempted to discuss strategy with Parizeau. At the last minute, however, Pari-zeau decided to set aside the written conciliatory remarks that had been pre-pared for him.[49]

The Yes supporters were very animated during Parizeau's speech, and although he only spoke briefly, chanting, singing, and cheering continuously interrupted him. Parizeau began his address by acknowledging that the refer-endum had gone down to defeat, then said, "Let's talk about us. Sixty percent of us voted in favor."[50] The crowd cheered. Then, after stating that the sepa-ratists would not "wait for another fifteen years" before the next referendum, Parizeau made the following statement: "But what has happened is wonderful. In one meeting after the next, people were saying that the future of their coun-try wasn't all that important, but more and more of them were coming along and were saying we want a country of our own, and we will get it. We will end up with our own country. It's true. It is true that we have been defeated, but basically by what? By money and by the ethnic vote. Basically that's it." The remainder of his speech was devoted to a reiteration of the fact that sixty per-cent of the francophones ("us") had voted for secession and that "solidarity" was "picking up speed." He concluded by listing a large number of groups who had joined the Yes camp, and conspicuously absent from his list were large corpo-rations, anglophones, and allophones.

But it was Parizeau's comment about "the ethnic vote" that would ulti-mately prove to be the most controversial. In a veritable explosion of criti-cism, reactions by reporters and political commentators immediately after his speech were universally negative, as were reactions in the French and English presses the following day. When the speech ended, the CBC news commen-tary began with a reporter noting the "money and ethnic vote remark" as being particularly offensive. Another reporter followed by remarking, "Mr. Parizeau also said at the beginning of his speech that sixty percent of *us* voted Yes. The history of Quebec, in many quarters over many years, has been a story about us and them, and who is a Quebecker and who is not a Quebecker, and it's a great sensitivity in Quebec, and Quebeckers have great difficulty talking about this and dealing with this because on the official level Quebec politicians have always told the rest of the province that if you pay taxes in Quebec and if you live in Quebec then you are a Quebecker." Another reporter representing the separatists stated that "Mr. Parizeau [was] pathetic. His words, to me, do not ring true. This is not how nationalists have envisioned Quebec. Nationalists have envisioned Quebec in a much more pluralist way, and in terms of leadership obviously here Mr. Parizeau is not leading the nationalist movement I do know." Yet another separatist stated that "what Mr. Parizeau did tonight was an appeal to ethnic nationalism which is really out of tune with the modern nationalism that has evolved." All in all, each of the respondents argued that Parizeau had made a terrible error, even though the Canadian presses reported the following day that in fact Parizeau had spoken the truth inasmuch as large corporate donations had been provided in support of the No side and that the "ethnic vote" had indeed been the principal factor in the referendum's defeat.

Responses to Parizeau's remarks in Canadian newspapers, regardless of the facts, were no kinder. The front page story in the Quebec paper *La Presse* discussed how, in the morning after the address, Parizeau "had to undergo a certain displeasure on the part of the most influential ministers meeting in the priorities committee" and that "certain deputies said frankly that Parizeau had to leave after such an outburst."[51] Additionally, *La Presse* was inundated with calls and letters of protest against Parizeau's remarks, many from secessionist supporters. Interestingly, many of the comments appearing in the newspapers were not so much concerned with the actual ethnic nationalist message conveyed by Parizeau, but with the "image" that such remarks would project.[52] Donald McKenzie, echoing the remarks of secessionist critics, noted, "The *Parti Québécois* has gone to great lengths in recent years to win over cultural communities to its cause. The PQ has gained some credibility with ethnic groups but is still viewed as an ethnocentric party."[53] Therefore, according to McKenzie, while Parizeau was factually correct in his claims, numerically speaking, such a "swipe" was a "no-no" because it gave renewed credence to the concerns that the separatist movement was based on ethnicity.

What can be witnessed in the rejection of Parizeau's address is the shifting movement of strategic remembrance of Quebec separatism away from the worn-out and increasingly suspect colonial arguments (the descendants of New France must preserve their culture from English cultural and economic hegemony) and toward strategic multiculturalism. That is, in response to the strategic multiculturalism and bilingualism of the federal government, Quebec would turn from ethnic nationalism to strategic multiculturalism and monolingualism.

As further evidence of this shift in strategic memory, less than a year after Parizeau's resignation, his successor, Bouchard, gave one of several addresses designed specifically for the non-francophone community entitled "Quebeckers Must Not Forget How to Live Together."[54] In that address, Bouchard articulated a *Québécois* identity based on multiculturalism and Quebec citizenship because, he argued, "We [Quebeckers] have to create a new atmosphere" based upon "a better understanding of how linguistic and cultural diversity make our metropolis vibrant and unique."[55] Bouchard additionally commented, "It should be known that the Quebec nationalism that we are building no longer defines itself as that of French-Canadians, but as that of all Quebeckers; it no longer seeks homogeneity but it embraces diversity and pluralism; it no longer focuses on political aims alone, but is also concerned with social and cultural issues that bind us all."[56] According to Bouchard, then, the "new" *Québécois* identity—that is, the new imagined community being articulated by the provincial leaders of Quebec—is multicultural. Seen in this light, Parizeau's address was dramatically rejected because it continued to articulate a vision of national identity that alienated the non-francophone population living within Quebec. Parizeau's dominant strategy of remembrance, borrowed from the long history of real and imagined English colonial oppression in Canada, had apparently outlived its usefulness.

### Strategic Multiculturalism and Globalization

The contextual analysis of controversial speech is an approach to discourse based in part on the assumption that sometimes certain truths cannot be publicly stated. In this instance, Parizeau could not say that non-francophones had cost the *Québécois* (whoever they were) their own country. Parizeau's address was dramatically rejected by federalists because of its exclusionary characterization of an ethnic-nationalism that created a dichotomy between an "us" (rising middle-class francophones) and "them" (multinational corporations, anglophones, and ethnic minorities); whereas separatists rejected the address because it exposed an ethnic nationalist strategy of remembrance no longer of use for the separatists' political agenda. While Bouchard made his "white race" remarks just weeks before the referendum, other actions both before and after indicate his superior sensitivity to the need for a shift of strategy.

Read generously, one could argue that the secessionists had "learned their lesson" and turned away from ethnic nationalism toward multiculturalism because of a genuine desire to be democratically inclusive. More skeptically, however, one could argue that the secessionists had merely become strategically multicultural to further the goal of gaining independence from federal Canada in order to more locally manage and efficiently compete in the global economy. Perhaps the federal government was also engaging in a "strategic" biculturalism in order to maximize federal state power at the expense of the provinces, and the liberal policies related to individual rights were simply a means of atomizing co-cultures living within Canada. Charles Taylor, for example, holds that "the supposedly neutral set of difference-blind principles of the politics of equal dignity is in fact a reflection of one hegemonic [English] culture. . . . [C]onsequently, the supposedly fair and difference-blind society is . . . itself highly discriminatory."[57]

Masao Miyoshi goes so far as to suggest that political liberalism itself may in fact be the ultimate multicultural mask for the leveling and homogenization of culture and the globalization of transnational corporate colonialism based on neo-liberal economic policies, although ethnic nationalist communitarianism may be no better, due to its historically proven potential for turning into aggressive national chauvinism.[58] If Miyoshi is correct, a crucial question is how to balance the globalization of the economy with the survival of local culture and history.

Undoubtedly there are many *Québécois* separatists who truly value the uniqueness of French Canadian culture and nonetheless believe in an imagined community where members can be both *Québécois* and multicultural. It is possible, in other words, that some nationalists envision a nation of Quebec that assimilates its citizens into a pluralistic francophone society that, while respecting the French language above all else, is nonetheless multicultural. Still, it is difficult to understand why secession would necessarily follow from such a vision, especially given pan-Canadian liberal federalism and the present balance of power between the provinces and the federal government. If the Canadian federation is already multicultural and bilingual, and if Quebec already possesses the constitutional right to preserve French Canadian culture and the French language, then why continue attempting to secede?

As we have seen, English Canadians maintained economic control within Quebec well into the twentieth century, and it was only after the successes of the Quiet Revolution and the rise of French power that federalists such as Trudeau attempted to articulate pan-Canadian identity as bilingual and multicultural. With this in mind, both federal multiculturalism and *Québécois* multiculturalism may be viewed as strategies, moves in the vast power struggle of the political economy. This is not equally to suggest, however, that strategic multiculturalism is necessarily a bad thing, for even a strategic multiculturalism is arguably better than an overt colonial ethnic nationalism. And yet, what if strategic multiculturalism is simply a new kind of imagined community that, by atomizing all cultural affiliations, sets the stage for a contemporary form of corporate colonialism?

Regardless of whether such scenarios are plausible, the Canadian case suggests that there is a strong relationship between the shifting nature of imagined community in Canada and its relationship to shifting balances of power within the Canadian federation, and between other competing states in our increasingly transnational economy. It also reinforces the claim that public discourse can be both truthful and transgressive and that discourse related to the public articulation of imagined community is distorted by the politics of memory. Imagined community can serve as a weapon in economic struggles and can easily devolve into a xenophobic and ethnocentric motive for the marginalization of others. Such uses of collective identity can occur in the most prosperous and relatively democratic of settings as well as in the poorest and least democratic. Social critics would do well to recognize that national identities are discursively contested, and they should seek to continue investigating the rhetorical processes through which those identities are created, maintained, and transformed.

CHAPTER FIVE

# Strategic Memory,
# National Identity, World Order

Almost a century ago, Vladimir Lenin argued that nationalism was the direct
result of economic inequalities between states.[1] Political theorists more recently
have argued that, given the *fact* of human inequality, the central questions facing those investigating nationalism and world order are on how to manage the
violence that accompanies that inequality. Are some forms of national identity
better at managing the violence of inequality than others? Are some strategies
of remembrance better than others? How can one tell? What are some of the
relationships between national identity construction as a rhetorical phenomenon, as a symbolic process of persuasion, and the overall material quality of
global community?

   To begin investigating such questions, examples of recent battles over
national identity in Germany, Russia, and Canada have been offered. Together,
they show that the analysis of controversial state discourse reveals competing
accounts of national identity with real political consequences. Analysing competing characterizations reveals in turn the various narrative omissions they
require, which in turn helps us reflect more precisely upon the political functions and consequences of those accounts. Through comparative case studies
we are also better equipped to analyze the construction of national imaginaries
as they unfold rhetorically.[2] Most important, we are simultaneously provided
with a catalogue of strategies of remembrance and, hopefully, a better understanding of the types of communities those strategies promote.

   The rhetorical dimension of national belonging undoubtedly remains a very
powerful force in both state politics and international relations. Different symbolic accounts of the nation's character, social philosophers concur, have very
real political consequences. Frederick Dolan maintains that "the most fateful
characteristic" of the contemporary world order is "the replacement of experience by fiction," and that those who would seek to deal with the violence of
inequality must first deal with the fabrication of collective identities. According
to Dolan, "Ideology and the atomization of individuals combine . . . to form a
'fictitious world,' one that replaces the real world constituted in a genuine public sphere."[3] Ernst Cassirer was equally concerned about the relationship
between mythology and community in *The Myth of the State*, arguing that the

entire history of Western political theory was nothing less than a struggle with mythology, or at least over the right use of mythology.[4] In his sweeping historical review, Cassirer observed that, generally speaking, in prosperous times the power of mythology recedes, but in bad times demagogues can easily prey upon the imaginations of the people.

While the quest for a "genuine public sphere" and "the right mix of realism and myth" may be utopian, it is surely not unreasonable to claim that there are more and less genuine public spheres and more and less productive myths. The studies here have suggested as much. Less "genuine" public spheres and less "healthy" myths appear to be those where the fabrication of national identity is based on particularly egregious absences and significant distortions of political realities. More "genuine" public spheres and "healthier" myths appear to be those where the fabrication of national identity is accompanied by incessant discursive and institutional efforts at uncovering the absences and distortions that invariably accompany articulations of collective identity.

Chantal Mouffe provides useful guidance when discussing identity ethics. For her, "the political community is crucial, but it should be conceived as a discursive surface and not as an empirical referent," and "what is really at stake in the question of pluralism is power and antagonism and their ineradicable nature."[5] "The main question of democratic politics becomes, therefore, not how to eliminate power, but how to constitute forms of power which are compatible with democratic values."[6] In the preceding cases, the political community has been conceptualized as having both a material history as well as a "discursive surface" where characterizations of the nation's identity have been variously compatible with democratic values and processes. For if one considers a relatively democratic public sphere as one where political motives are available for reflexive critique, where the public is well informed about crucial political realities, and where the unjust marginalization of others is minimized, then articulations of collective national identity that suppress significant political facts, misdirect the public's attention from crucial political issues, or arbitrarily demonize others in order to achieve solidarity are antidemocratic.

### Toward a "Healthy" Conception of National Identity

Collective identities, constructed primarily in response to economic exigencies or historical traumas, are generally tools of the state in the consolidation of power.[7] However, rather than simply being tools, they are also historically developed and politically consequential symbolic constructions citizens are enmeshed in, and understanding their variety is an important step in connecting national identity to world order.

Not only is there a wide variety of specific strategies for public memory, there are also different ways of conceptualizing national identity that have equally profound, if variously "healthy," political consequences. Anthony Smith, in a survey of theories of nationalism, explains how there are basically three theoretical approaches (and hence political practices) related to the "origin" of nations: romantic, situational, and historical/symbolic.[8] *Romantic* theorists maintain that each nation has a unique and immutable essence and that each nation must "realize" its unique personality. Guided by such an understanding, they seek to "protect" their nation from being "polluted" by "others." Unfortunately, such "romantic" assumptions generally lead to unreflexive, undemocratic, and hence "unhealthy" communities (e.g., Nazi Germany). *Situational* theorists, conversely, argue that the nation "is a matter of attitudes, perceptions and sentiments that are necessarily fleeting and mutable, varying with the particular situation of the subject." The primary problem with this approach is that situational theorists believe that national identities shift as people's immediate situation changes. National identity, therefore, is almost completely fictional. Smith observes that such a perspective "makes it possible for ethnicity to be used 'instrumentally' to further individual or collective interests, particularly of competing elites who need to mobilize large followings to support goals in the struggle for power."[9] This is Nietzsche's "monumental history" coupled with intentional identity entrepreneurship.

Smith goes on, however, to argue that between these two theoretical perspectives is a more moderate and healthier approach to national identity construction that stresses both the historical-material and symbolic-cultural attributes of collective identity. According to this third theoretical perspective, the collective identities upon which national affiliations are built are neither pure "essences" nor pure fabrications from state leaders. Instead, they are "co-constructed" by state leaders and publics out of available historical and symbolic-cultural resources for competing instrumental purposes under emerging circumstances, and the purposes and rhetorical strategies of these "co-constructions" are variously useful and harmful. This third theoretical perspective is clearly the one taken here, where it is a given that unique historical, economic, political, and/or emotional pressures place ideological constraints on public speakers providing characterization of the national persona. Characterizations that work against either the dominant instrumental purposes of the state and/or the narrative expectations of the public become controversial. The constraints, therefore, result in a politics of memory based upon quasi-fictional but politically consequential characterizations of what it means to be a citizen of the state.

Rather than assuming that national identity is a purely "natural" process from the bottom up, or a purely manipulative process from the top down, national character is most appropriately conceptualized as a constant tension between motivated interpretations of the past and motivated visions of the present and future. By working to identify narrative omissions related to dominant characterizations of the nation's identity, social and rhetorical critics provide a perspective that purely historical approaches do not. Historical descriptions of state actions are thereby complemented with analyses of the ways in which various discourses prompted, or at least contributed to, those actions.

The preceding chapters have shown that articulations of national identity in West Germany, Russia, and Quebec were accompanied by politically significant absences. In West Germany those absences concerned the causes for, continuities of, and responsibility for, National Socialism. National Socialists had suddenly become democrats in West Germany, and East Germans suddenly became responsible for all the evils of fascism (now communism). An important point for those considering the unfolding nature of the new world order is not that there were many innocent Germans unduly lumped together with the guilty as perpetrators, for surely that was the case, but that the fascist potential of "market democracies" was diluted by associating all the perpetrators with communist East Germany.

In Russia those absences also concerned the use of the term *democracy*, when few if any of the people employing the term were particularly determined to strengthen the rule of law or share power in any meaningful sense. In fact, the "democrats" were usually ex-Soviet officials seeking to reconsolidate state power in a form that would best protect their economic interests at the expense of the average citizen, so democracy and the Soviets were *truly* not compatible because there were really no democrats in significant positions of power in Russia. Another important point here for those concerned with the relationship between strategic memory and world order is that the easy equation of free markets and democracy is a deceptive one. Healthy democracies require an economy governed by the rule of law, and the failures of reform in Russia should be an object lesson in what "market democracies" actually require.

In Quebec the absences concerned the neo-racist foundation of *Québécois* identity and the historical importance of that ethnic identity in economic battles within the federation. Yet another important point here for those concerned with national identity and world order is that separatist struggles, often triggered by the pressures of economic globalization, really have little to do with the protection of culture and instead are best seen as attempts to use culture as an economic weapon.

The three studies have also shown that these politically significant absences, these motivated accounts of history, oftentimes reflect the fact that crucial political realities are being ignored or hidden that result in less "healthy" states. In both West Germany and Quebec, national newspapers critiquing Jenninger and Parizeau noted that neither of the men had actually said anything untrue; rather, what they said was inappropriate. Still, the plain truth could not be spoken. The surviving National Socialists and their sympathizers and the ethnic basis of Quebec nationalism simply could not be publicly recognized (although there were in fact surviving National Socialists and their sympathizers, and many of those seeking a sovereign Quebec did so to protect their interests as the descendants of the New French). The situation in Russia was somewhat different. There, Yeltsin attempted to falsely dissociate himself from "the Soviets," and in claiming the mantle of democracy for himself inspired the rage of not only his political opponents (who also wanted to wear that mantle), but of the actual democratic political reformers who had lost touch with Yeltsin upon his ascension to the presidency. Here, Yeltsin's own ties with the Soviet system and the general absence of democratic process was hidden by the discourse of democracy itself.

Finally, these analyses of dramatically rejected speeches also help to show how "codes of appropriateness" are instrumentally motivated (if ideologically constrained): in West Germany public remembrance of National Socialism ultimately was in the service of reunification; in Russia democratic terminology was used in the service of antidemocratic measures and a criminal takeover of the natural and financial resources of the state; and in Quebec articulations of national identity appear to have been in the service of maximizing the economic power of the rising francophone middle class. Obviously these are variously "healthy" motives for those concerned with the transformation and maintenance of world order.

### The Use and Abuse of National Identity

When one considers the general malleability of publics, as witnessed by the wide variety of national allegiances observable in the world today, rhetoric scholars cannot help but wonder about the ramifications of constructing publics in ways that may frequently, if not always, preclude certain politically significant issues from being publicly acknowledged and addressed. One of the key advantages of the contextual analysis of controversial speech, as we have seen, is its ability to identify what those unspeakable things are. Should the Germans, or world citizens in general, actively be considering the possible connections between capitalism and fascism? Should the Russians, or global citizens, be publicly debating the differences between concrete democratic market reform and corrupt forms of neo-liberal economic reform? Should the citizens of Quebec, or all "patriots," be able to better reflect upon the relationships among economic and cultural globalization, the emergence of the nation-state system, and identity entrepreneurship? Obviously they, and we, should.

Imagined communities can be co-constructed for a variety of purposes, and different kinds of absences reflect the kinds of action publics might be expected to engage in. In some ways, then, it is unfortunate that all three case studies found what are arguably serious and egregious absences, for such an outcome could give the impression that all national identities require absences that misdirect the public's attention from crucial issues that need to be debated in order to ensure the overall health and well being of states. While that may be the case, it is more likely that *all* national identities require the suppression of politically consequential facts but that not all of those suppressed facts are equally egregious.

National identity is arguably capable of attaining both a "healthy" and an "unhealthy" state, and nationalism may be used as a tool (albeit ideologically constrained) for a variety of useful and harmful purposes. However, as the Russian and Canadian studies indicate, it is equally likely that the nation-state is in unwitting ways the product of global economic forces that are insufficiently understood. The early nineteenth century Russian political theorist Nikolai Bukharin argued that nationalism should be generally acknowledged as an effective co-opting device for the bourgeoisie,[10] and Leon Trotsky argued that the state always is a tool in the hands of the ruling forces and that national sentiment is their primary means of consolidating power.[11] These bleak "situationalist" perspectives, however, are countered by Smith, who points out that, "We could, equally, catalogue the benign effects of nationalism: its defence of minority cultures; its rescue of 'lost' histories and literatures; its inspiration for cultural renascences; its resolution of 'identity crisis'; its legitimation of community and social solidarity; its inspiration to resist tyranny; its ideal of popular sovereignty and collective mobilization; even the motivation of self-sustaining economic growth."[12] Unfortunately, the three cases explored here do not seem to be the most useful sites for defending the potentially positive, capacity generating functions of nationalism, save perhaps for the strategic multiculturalism developing in Quebec despite the wishes of nationalists bent on maximizing local economic power through French, rather than bilingual, language laws coupled with incessant threats of secession.

Again, Smith provides a useful, if somewhat oversimplified, typology for comparing different forms of nationalism by maintaining that there are two basic types of national identities: "Western" (civic/economic) and "Asian" (ethnic/cultural). According to Smith, "Western" models of the nation are based on historic territory, a legal-political community, legal-political equality of members, and common civic culture and ideology, whereas "Asian" models of the nation are characterized by common descent, popular mobilization, vernacular languages, and shared customs and traditions. The former might be characterized as *constitutional nationalisms* (where civil rights outweigh ethnicity and cultural membership), while the latter could be characterized as *communitarian nationalisms* (where ethnicity and cultural membership outweigh "liberal" civil rights).[13]

Such a clear distinction, however, between "Western" and "Asian" forms of nation building are problematic, as Smith admits. Instead, it is more accurate to say that national identities display each of the characteristics of the two general types in various proportions. In National Socialist Germany, for example, ethnic identity became the container for the economic policies of the state, while civic and economic identity came to the fore in 1945 as capitalist democracy began its fight against the "Red menace." In Russia, an imperial Soviet identity became the collective container for the multicultural federation in its doomed world-historical battle with the nationalist capitalists, until the term "democrat" became more useful during the rampant identity entrepreneurship of the early 1990s in helping to push through "triumphant" neo-liberal market reforms and redistribute economic and political power in the post-Soviet world. In Quebec, an ethnic identity had been of great political use for over twenty years of nation building, but by 1995 it had become an awkward relic in the rhetorical battle for a multicultural collective identity to be wielded for an ultimately economic purpose.

These ever shifting proportional variations (civic, economic, cultural, ethnic) have a direct impact on the kinds of absences constraining public discourses and the kinds of publics (and the motives for actions on the part of socially constructed subjects within those publics) likely to be expected from those variations. Smith's simple bifurcation is nonetheless a useful starting point for an investigation into different configurations of national identities, since in West Germany and Quebec, both "Western" nations, there are many "Asian" characteristics; and in Russia, ambivalent in its Eurasianism, there are many "Western" characteristics. In each state there appears to be an ongoing struggle between constitutional patriotism based upon the rule of law, civil rights, freedom of speech and assembly, and effective competition on the one hand and allegiances based upon respect for and protection of unique ethnic and cultural characteristics on the other. West Germany and Quebec are involved in forms of government based upon relatively democratic constitutional law, yet both, at some time in their history, sought to strengthen national identity through educational and cultural ministries, language policies, and the promotion of issues related to descent. In Russia, a state where the rule of law has always been weak and constitutions have served as rubber stamps for "Party boss" dictates, the ethnic dimensions of Russian identity have rarely been politically expedient, and yet constitutional patriotism has not taken root.

Investigations into national identity construction suggest that there are other significant problems associated with both "Western" and "Asian" models. Neither model addresses the economic/material conditions influencing both camps. There are other unseen dangers. Constitutional patriotism and capitalist democracy potentially lead to the atomization of subjects, the commodification of culture,[14] and may ultimately be in the service of corporate neocolonialism that will soon overwhelm local representative governments.[15] Behind the "mask" of individual freedom may lurk a systemic censorship (not state censorship but the "censorship" of a market logic) and an uncivil capitalism that "capitalizes" on the lack of community affiliation and group solidarity usually found in publics fabricated around ethnic and cultural issues. The collapse of the collective identities of the world into smaller and smaller units, according to such a view, is simply a reflection and consequence of the atomizing power of our contemporary economic environment. In a different, but equally problematic manner, "Asian" (ethnic/cultural) nationalism potentially leads to the demonization and scapegoating of others, violent xenophobia, overt censorship, and egregious state constrictions on the public sphere that allow neo-feudal lords to maintain unjust economic and political privileges.

Yet another reason both ethnic and civic forms of nation building are potentially dangerous is that both allow for the manipulation of public consciousness: market societies produce mass messages where the primary goal is profit rather than information (to the detriment of critical thinking), and totalitarian societies produce mass messages where the primary goal is the unification of public opinion at the expense of critical thinking (and access to information). In neither system is the primary goal of public discourse to maximally inform the citizenry in order to create healthy public spheres or to facilitate the highest quality decision-making. The key, perhaps, is to find the kinds of community fictions and supporting institutional structures that will defend constitutional patriotism and local representation while protecting against the intrusions of relatively unhealthy forms of public memory and the institutional problems such strategies create.

The analysis of failed speeches articulating national identity, arguably more than any other approach to the subject, reveals how there is an intimate relationship between narratives of public belonging, economic processes, and political communities. National identities articulated by state leaders, while clearly constrained by hegemonic strategies of remembrance and oppositional voices, proactively contribute to the construction, maintenance, and transformation of those identities. Furthermore, national identities are created and transformed through strategies of remembrance where the goal is oftentimes to maximize "national" or group self-interest rather than to build more just democratic states or a more harmonious global community. In West Germany, the concern was not to deal effectively with the root causes of fascism, but rather to "emerge from the shadow of Hitler" in order to get on with the business of democratic capitalism (regardless of the possible affiliations between capitalism and fascism). In Russia the concern was to reestablish power in a weakened state, to push through corrupt neo-liberal market reforms, and redistribute power, not to concretely transform the political system of Russia in a manner that would ensure the emergence of a viable market democracy. In Quebec, the concern was not to deal openly and frankly with the racial, cultural, and economic discord within the Canadian federation, but to deny the ethnic basis of secessionist arguments in order to maximize the economic power of descendants of the French Canadians.

### Critiquing the Construction of National Identity

A complex relationship exists, therefore, among characterizations of national identity and motivated narrative and political absences, among the tensions between different theories of the nation, among the tensions between ethnic, economic, civic, and cultural aspects of national identity, and among the economic incentives behind the transition from monarchy to nationalism and from nationalism to globalization. Here, however, each of these issues has been touched upon in ways that provide criteria for critiquing the fabrication of publics. West Germany, Russia, and Quebec provide useful anti-models for the construction of a post-national form of collective identity construction more appropriate for the increasingly interdependent global society. In those states, the discourses of victimage, democracy, and multiculturalism became masks for what were ultimately economic battles, yet the economic battles themselves remained publicly unaddressed (save partially in Quebec).

In Germany, Russia, and Canada, nation building arose primarily as a result of military conflicts and economic inequalities with other communities.

German nationalism was prompted in no small part by the French Revolution, a series of subsequent military defeats culminating in defeat in World War I, and perceived economic backwardness in relation to England and France. Russian nationalism has ever been a love/hate relationship with Western Europe, and Russians have always felt behind in the race of states. Quebec nationalism was prompted in part by military conflicts with the English and perceived economic backwardness in relation to English Canadians. In each case, political leaders mobilized national sentiment in order to remedy these perceived inequities. Therefore one criterion by which to judge nation-builders is their economic motivation. Whose economic interests are best served by the dominant strategy of remembrance?

Unfortunately, the essentializing and "ethnic" tendencies at the heart of most nationalist movements, especially when combined with interstate military alliances and the anti-community dimensions of market economies, suggest the lingering threat of world war. However, as the situation in Canada suggests, there is the possibility of a stage in collective identity construction where identity politics are transformed into strategic multiculturalism (where the state agrees to respect marginalized groups in order to maintain power). Although strategic multiculturalism may yet be another mask for the maintenance of political and economic hegemony, it would still appear to be one of the more enabling and less constraining forms of collective identity currently available. Therefore, another criterion by which to judge national identity is the degree to which it is a xenophobic ethnic or cultural nationalism based on romantic or situational theories, or a strategically multicultural constitutional patriotism based on historical/symbolic theories.

According to these first two criteria, "healthier" nationalisms would be led by leaders who publicly acknowledge and forthrightly debate their economic motives while stressing a form of collective identity not based on the demonization of an Other or the erasure of crucial political realities. Of course, given Wallerstein's observation that the primary role of the state is maximizing the economic power of certain select citizens, and given the case studies analyzed here, such public economic acknowledgements and debates are unlikely. Furthermore, since a major public argument for "sovereignty" requires the establishment of a difference, there is always the risk of demonization.

Clearly, outcomes will be different in each state. The dialogic struggle between the federal and provincial levels of government in Canada led to the development of strategic multiculturalism on both levels, but in Russia that struggle led to the reestablishment of a "strong executive" more interested in supporting criminal business oligarchs than establishing the rule of law. Since the difference between the two outcomes may be due to the relative strength of democratic political structures in Canada and the relative absence of such political structures in Russia, such distinctions suggest other, perhaps an even more fundamental criterion for "healthy" nation building: the relative presence or absence of complex institutional infrastructures capable of maintaining democratic markets and institutionalized self-critiques designed to ensure those infrastructures exist. This would require that, instead of the all too easy equation in U.S. public discourse between "free markets" and "democracy," the institutional requirements for *true* democracy be incessantly and productively debated publicly. Does the state have a strong and independent judiciary? Is the public sphere, including of course the press, complex enough to be adequately free from either corporate or political influence? Do laws adequately maintain fair competition, civil and human rights, and a separation and balance of powers? Are there multiple parties and frequent elections? Most important, are there frequent and meaningful opportunities for the public critique of state narratives and state policies?

When constructing a collective identity, if the correct democratic political conditions are in place (a relatively productive identity ethic, a relatively free press, a relatively strong middle class, relatively just and fairly applied laws, a relatively informed citizenry, a relatively just distribution of wealth, etc.), then maximum public competition and discursive conflict are generally good. Consensus, however, especially in the absence of those (relative) conditions, is disaster. "There is no ideal community or subject," notes Honi Fern Haber, "which is not subject to deconstruction. If this is suppressed, then community or the ideal of a 'normal subject' is indeed repressive. But it is repressive because it presents the subject and community to be something they are not. A politics of difference does not then imagine that all conflict should be resolved. There will always be groups [who are] forced to the margins. What it hopes for, however, is the fluidity of positions of power; it hopes to encourage the proliferation of voices."[16] Building upon Haber's theory, then, a "healthy" national identity would finally be one that fosters and yet can justly sustain a proliferation of voices, of subject positions, of sites of knowledge/power, whereas an "unhealthy" national identity would be one in which the state so restricts the public sphere as to limit the voice of the public to only one position or a few, or is capable of maintaining an egregious historical deception.

Kenneth Burke's analysis of Hitler's rhetoric is instructive when considering the value of national consensus. In an early warning to his American audience, Burke argued that, "Already, in many quarters of our country, we are 'beyond' the stage where we are being saved from Nazism by our *virtues*. And fascist integration is being staved off, rather, by the *conflicts among our vices*. Our vices cannot get together in a grand unified front of prejudices; and the result of this frustration, if or until they succeed in surmounting it, speaks, as the Bible might say, 'in the name of' democracy."[17] Fascism, then, or totalitarianism is associated with the unification of prejudice, or, in the terminology used here, with the success of a strategy of remembrance based upon unrecognized politically egregious absences. Later in his essay, Burke makes an additional comment that strikes at the heart of such a claim when he states that, "The desire for unity is genuine and admirable. The desire for national unity, in the present state of the world is genuine and admirable. But this unity, if attained on a deceptive basis, by emotional trickeries that shift our criticism from the accurate locus of our trouble, is no unity at all."[18]

But in these studies it appears that all national identities may be "deceptive" inasmuch as they "shift our criticism from the accurate locus" of the ultimate motives underlying their construction. Worse yet, when publics are unaware of those motives, the constraints imposed by strategies of remembrance go unrecognized. Germans on both the Left and the Right embraced Weizsäcker's address, even though it played directly into the hands of those who would deflect attention away from responsible critical analyses of National Socialism, and Western observers embraced Yeltsin as a great democrat when the association between neo-liberal economic reform and democracy was so strong that it effaced the actual weakening of the state and the relative absence of concrete democratic political reform.

In the end, it appears to be the case that the current state of national identity construction in such "advanced" countries as Germany, Russia, and Canada is far from "healthy," and the best form of national identity that can be hoped for given the current world order may be strategic multiculturalism and an ongoing and uphill struggle for constitutional patriotism. More likely than not, communal regeneration will never become unnecessary. Instead, we will need to find ways to manage the racism and economic advantage-taking that historically accompanies collective identity formation. By identifying those nation builders who construct collective identities based on public debates about economic motives, who encourage the proliferation of voices while simultaneously guarding against corporate colonialism or essentialist collectivism, who valorize the celebration of cultural diversity when that diversity is not won at the cost of demonization of the Other, who relatively accurately characterize historical conditions, who boldly support the rule of law, and who maintain an eternal vigilance over those incessantly marginalized by hegemonic articulations of collective belonging, rhetorical critics may be in a better position to understand the relationship between the negotiation of national identity and the construction of variously "healthy" publics.

By coming to a better understanding of the kinds of collective national identities constructed in different contexts, we will be in a better position to distinguish more clearly between "healthy" and "unhealthy" forms of national identity as they are unfolding. Therefore, comparative studies of nation-building should therefore continue until those strategies of remembrance and those forms of state are identified that best protect the interests of those who are incessantly marginalized, that allow those marginalized voices to participate meaningfully in the construction of state policy, and that maximize economic and political opportunities for all citizens. So informed, political activists and government officials, as well as theorists, must find ways to work proactively toward the construction of state systems fostering those features of national identity that maximize universal human capacities while minimizing unnecessary constraints on human action.

There are many dangers facing our increasingly interdependent world arising from nation building, and given the fact that communal regeneration in the form of ethnic, neo-colonial corporate, and fundamentalist nationalisms are proliferating, there are daunting challenges ahead. While rhetoricians perhaps can do little to stop the kinds of economic and ideational violence that wracks humankind, as Burke's ignored critique of Hitler written in advance of World War II so poignantly testifies, the development of critical tools for evaluating national identity construction would be unlikely to exacerbate such violence. In the end, it is humans who create states, and in the end it is humans who will have to make them more humane. The contextual analysis of controversial speech related to national identity, and the isolation of strategies of remembrance that it enables, is a productive move in the eventual production of more humane systems of human governance, and the development of more humane guidelines for the public negotiation of national identity.

# NOTES

## Chapter 1 — The Rhetorical Dimensions of National Identity

1. Erik Ringmar, "Nationalism: The Idiocy of Intimacy," *British Journal of Sociology* 49 (1998): 537.

2. Rhetoric scholars do tangentially touch on national identity through their discussions on memorialization and the construction of audiences and publics. Maurice Charland, "Constitutive Rhetoric: The Case of the Peuple Québécois," *Quarterly Journal of Speech* 73 (1987): 133–50; Carole Blair, Marsha Jeppeson, and Enrico Pucci Jr., "Public Memorialization in Postmodernity: The Vietnam Veterans Memorial as Prototype," *Quarterly Journal of Speech* 73 (1991): 263–88; Michael C. McGee, "In Search of 'The People': A Rhetorical Alternative," Quarterly Journal of Speech 61 (1975): 235–49; Michael McGee and Martha Anne Martin, "Public Knowledge and Ideological Argumentation," *Communication Monographs* 50 (1983): 47–65; Raymie McKerrow, "Critical Rhetoric: Theory and Praxis," *Communication Monographs* 56 (1989): 91–111; Raymie McKerrow, "Argument Communities," in *Perspectives on Argumentation*, ed. Robert Trapp and Janice Schuetz (Prospect Heights, Ill.: Waveland Press, 1990), 27–40.

3. The literature on nationalism outside of rhetoric studies is vast. Frequently cited texts include Elie Kedourie, *Nationalism* (Cambridge, Mass.: Blackwell, 1993); Hugh Seton-Watson, *Nations and States* (Boulder, Colo.: Westview Press, 1977); John Breuilly, *Nationalism and the State* (Manchester: Manchester University Press, 1982); Benedict Anderson, *Imagined Communities* (New York: Verso, 1991); Liah Greenfield, *Nationalism: Five Roads to Modernity* (Cambridge, Mass.: Harvard University Press, 1992); Anthony Giddens, *The Nation-State and Violence* (Cambridge, Mass: Polity Press, 1985); and John Hutchinson and Anthony D. Smith, eds., *Nationalism* (New York: Oxford University Press, 1994). Other useful introductions to national identity include Michael Billig, *Banal Nationalism* (Thousand Oaks, Calif.; Sage, 1995); Anthony D. Smith, *Nations and Nationalism in a Global Era* (Cambridge, Mass.: Polity Press, 1995); and Craig Calhoun, *Nationalism* (Minneapolis: University of Minnesota Press, 1997).

4. The wide variety of texts related to the discursive construction of identities include Michel Foucault, *The Archaeology of Knowledge* (New York: Pantheon Books, 1972); John Shotter and Kenneth J. Gergen, eds., *Texts of Identity* (London: Sage Publications, 1989); Charles Taylor, *Sources of the Self: The Making of Modern Identity* (Cambridge, Mass.: Cambridge University Press, 1989); Judith Butler, *Gender Trouble: Feminism and the Subversion of Identity* (New York: Routledge, 1990); William Connolly, *Identity/Difference: Democratic Negotiations of Political Paradox* (Ithaca, N.Y.:

Cornell University Press, 1991); and John Rajchman, ed., *The Identity in Question* (New York: Routledge, 1995). Greenfield's *Nationalism: Five Roads To Modernity* (1992) provides an excellent historical comparison of national identity development but is not focused on the rhetorical processes involved in emergent national identity construction.

5. Rodney Bruce Hall, *National Collective Identity: Social Constructs and International Systems* (New York: Columbia University Press, 1999), 28.

6. For descriptions of democratic and authoritarian political cultures respectively, see Ernesto Laclau and Chantal Mouffe, *Hegemony and Socialist Strategy* (New York: Verso, 1985), 149–93; Ulf Hedetoft, "National Identity and Mentalities of War in Three EC Countries," *Journal of Peace Research* 30 (1993): 281–300.

7. Hayden White, "Historical Emplotment and the Problem of Truth," in *Probing the Limits of Representation: Nazism and the 'Final Solution,'* ed. Saul Friedlander (Cambridge, Mass.: Harvard University Press, 1992), 37–44; Robert J. Cox, "Memory, Critical Theory, and the Argument from History," *Argumentation and Advocacy* 27 (1990): 1–13. A strategy of remembrance is a form of political memory or a motivated account of history requiring that certain politically consequential things not be said in order to maintain the narrative coherence of the account.

8. The growth of nationalism and the nation-state in Europe is the subject of abundant research; see, for example, Anderson, *Imagined Communities*, 1983; Ernest Gellner, *Nations and Nationalism* (Oxford: Basil Blackwell, 1983); Eric Hobsbawm, *Nations and Nationalism since 1780: Programme, Myth, Reality* (New York: Cambridge University Press, 1990); Seton-Watson, *Nations and States*, 1977. For an introduction to contemporary identity theory, see Rajchman, *Identity in Question*, 1995.

9. For an interesting discussion of the creation of Siam/Thailand under such influences, see Winichakul Thongchai, *Siam Mapped: A History of the Geo-Body of a Nation* (Honolulu: University of Hawaii Press, 1994).

10. Hall, *National Collective Identity*, 77–132; Roman Szporluk, *Communism and Nationalism: Karl Marx versus Friedrich List* (New York: Oxford University Press, 1988), 55–58.

11. Bruce G. Carruthers, *City of Capital: Politics and Markets in the English Financial Revolution* (Princeton, N.J.: Princeton University Press, 1996), 1–26.

12. Szporluk, *Communism and Nationalism*, 108.

13. William Bloom, *Personal Identity, National Identity, and International Relations* (Cambridge: Cambridge University Press, 1990), 64–71.

14. Henry Kissinger, *Diplomacy* (New York: Simon & Schuster, 1994), 30; Hobsbawm, *Nations and Nationalism since 1780*, 131–33.

15. Ernest Gellner, *Nations and Nationalism*, 44. The competition between those seeking a new nation-state and those seeking to maintain an existing national identity is exemplified in the struggle between regional and federal leaders in the Russian and Canadian studies in chapters 3 and 4. The tendency of existing states to absorb smaller cultural communities is discussed in Walker Connor, "Nation-Building or Nation-Destroying," *World Politics* 24 (1972): 519–55.

16. Ethnic identities based on shared physical traits, according to the theories of identity summarized in the following sections, are just as "fictional" as national identities.

17. Gellner, *Nations and Nationalism*, 57; Richard Sennett, *The Fall of Public Man* (New York: W. W. Norton, 1977), 47–63.

18. Anthony Smith, *National Identity* (Las Vegas: University of Nevada Press, 1991), 43–70.

19. This simple dualism is complicated by concrete examples, but it helps to illustrate two fundamentally opposed trajectories for collective identity. See Smith, *National Identity*, 8–22.

20. Honi Fern Haber, *Beyond Postmodern Politics* (New York: Routledge, 1994), 116.

21. Friedrich Nietzsche, "On Truth and Lie in an Extra-Moral Sense," in *Philosophy and Truth: Selections From Nietzsche's Notebooks of the Early 1970s*, translated and edited by Daniel Breazeale (Atlantic Highlands, N.J.: Humanities Press, 1979), 246–57; Michel Foucault, "What is Enlightenment?" in *The Foucault Reader*, ed. Paul Rabinow (New York: Pantheon, 1984), 32–50; Laclau and Mouffe, *Hegemony and Socialist Strategy*, 7–46, 149–94.

22. Louis Althusser, "Ideology and Ideological State Apparatuses," in *Critical Theory Since 1965*, ed. Hazard Adams and Leroy Searle (Tallahassee: Florida State University Press, 1986), 245. If for no other reason, national identities are particularly compelling because they are backed up by the power of the state.

23. Michel Foucault, "A Preface to Transgression," *Critique* (1963): 751–70; Jon Simons, *Foucault and the Political* (New York: Routledge, 1995), 89.

24. Connolly, *Identity/Difference*, 14.

25. This approach diverges in a significant way from Sloop's and Ono's (Sloop, John M. and Kent Ono, "Out-law Discourse: The Critical Politics of Material Judgement," *Philosophy and Rhetoric* 30 [1997]: 50–69) conception of out-law discourse. While out-law discourse and limit work converge around theories related to identity construction and democracy, out-law theory focuses on emancipatory rearticulations of nondominant discourses. Limit work, conversely, focuses on the analysis of transgressive dominant discourses and their relationship to shifting narrative articulations of imagined community.

26. Friedrich Nietzsche, *On the Advantage and Disadvantage of History For Life* (Indianapolis, Ind.: Hacket, 1980), 17.

27. Ibid., 17.

28. For a discussion of interpellation (i.e., the process of "hailing" the subject), see Stuart Hall, "Signification, Representation, Ideology: Althusser and the Post-Structuralist Debates," *Critical Studies in Mass Communication* 2 (1985): 94–112; Althusser, "Ideology," 1986.

29. Foucault provides another interpretation of Nietzsche's theory of history in his explication of "effective history"; see Michel Foucault, "Nietzsche, Genealogy, History," in *Foucault Reader*, ed. Paul Rabinow (New York: Pantheon Books, 1984), 86–90.

30. My most recent research also suggests that discourses emerging around sites of public protest also reveal competing characterizations with sufficient clarity to identify motivated narrative absences.

31. The term strategy does not mean to necessarily suggest intention. Just as the market has a "logic" of its own, just as reified institutional norms and practices are oftentimes beyond any subject's control, and just as our various language games make certain moves "make sense," the term strategy simply means the discourse "had" to change to fit the new scene. Truth or deception often has little to do with it. If political conditions are assumed to be x, then y policies must prevail. Discourses that best support favored policies become the new "strategies." However, the frameworks for interpreting political conditions are themselves saturated with hegemonic articulations; therefore, "appropriate" policy is also infused by a preexisting set of discourses.

### Chapter 2—National Identity in Pre-Unification West Germany

1. Charles S. Maier, *The Unmasterable Past: History, Holocaust, and German National Identity* (Cambridge, Mass.: Harvard University Press, 1988); Geoff Eley, "Nazism, Politics and Public Memory: Thoughts on the West German *Historikerstreit* 1986–1987," *Past and Present* 121 (1988): 171–208; Stefan Berger, "Historians and Nation-Building in Germany After Reunification," *Past and Present* 148 (1995): 187–222; Gregory Jusdanis, "Beyond National Culture?" *Boundary* 2 22 (1995): 23–60.

2. Heiko Girnth, "Einstellung und Einstellungsbekündung in der politischen Rede: Eine sprachwissenschaftliche Untersuchung der Rede Philipp Jenningers vom 10. November 1988," in *Europäische Hochschulschriften* (Frankfurt am Main: Peter Lang, 1993), 4.

3. For useful discussions of the events related to Bitburg, see Stephen Brockmann, "Bitburg Deconstruction," *Philosophical Forum* 17 (1986): 159–74; and Geoffrey Hartmann, ed., *Bitburg in Moral and Political Perspective* (Bloomington: University of Indiana Press, 1986). The literature on the *Historikerstreit* is extensive. *Forever in the Shadow of Hitler*, trans. James Knowlton and Truett Cates (Atlantic Highlands, N.J.: Humanities Press International, 1993) is a compilation of the principal texts of the debate and a translation of the original German edition compiled by Ernst Reinhard Piper entitled *Historikerstreit: Die Dokumentation der Kontroverse um die Einzigartigkeit der nationalsozialistischen Judenvernichtung* (Munich: Piper, 1987). See also Peter Baldwin, ed., *Reworking the Past: Hitler, the Holocaust, and the Historians' Debate* (Boston: Beacon Press, 1990).

4. For a discussion of some of the controversies surrounding Reagan's visit and the ways in which those conflicts were portrayed in the New York Times, see Kathryn M. Olson, "The Controversy over President Reagan's Visit to Bitburg: Strategies of Definition and Redefinition," *Quarterly Journal of Speech* 75 (1989): 129–51; and "The Function of Form in Newspapers' Political Conflict Coverage: *The New York Times'*

Shaping of Expectations in the Bitburg Controversy," *Political Communication* 12 (1995): 43–64.

5. An English version of Weizsäcker's address can be found in Hartmann, *Bitburg*, 262–73. A complete copy of the text in German can be found in Girnth, *Einstellung*, 277–98.

6. Hartmann, *Bitburg*, xv–xvi; Olson, "Controversy," 129–34.

7. Eley, "Nazism," 176.

8. Maier, *Unmasterable Past*, 10.

9. Brockmann, "Bitburg Deconstruction," 161.

10. Olson, "Controversy," 145–46.

11. Brockmann, "Bitburg Deconstruction," 163.

12. Hartmann, *Bitburg*, xiii.

13. Ibid., xiv. Olson ("Controversy," 141–46) also discusses how Reagan attempted to redefine the notion of "victims" prior to and during his Bitburg visit, equating the victims of National Socialism with National Socialist perpetrators.

14. Among those scholars who have investigated the denial of responsibility for National Socialism in Germany are Elizabeth Domansky, "'Kristallnacht,' the Holocaust and German Unity: The Meaning of November 9 as an Anniversary in Germany," *History & Memory* 4 (1992): 60–94; and Heiner Müller, "Germany's Identity Crisis," *New Perspectives Quarterly* 10 (1993): 16–19.

15. Martin Broszat, "A Plea for the Historicization of National Socialism," in *Reworking the Past: Hitler, the Holocaust, and the Historian's Debate*, ed. Peter Baldwin (Boston: Beacon Press, 1990), 79; Domansky, "Kristallnacht," 70.

16. Brockmann, "Bitburg Deconstruction," 170.

17. For example, see Joachim Fest, "Encumbered Remembrance: The Controversy About the Incomparability of National Socialist Crimes," *Forever in the Shadow of Hitler*, 63–71; and Ernst Nolte, "The Past That Will Not Pass: A Speech That Could Be Written but Not Delivered," *Forever in the Shadow of Hitler*, 18–23.

18. Jürgen Habermas, "A Kind of Settlement of Damages: The Apologetic Tendencies in German History Writing," in *Forever in the Shadow of Hitler*, 41; Maier, *Unmasterable Past*, 10.

19. Jürgen Kocka, "Hitler Should Not Be Repressed by Stalin and Pol Pot: On the Attempts of German Historians to Relativize the Enormity of the Nazi Crimes," in *Forever in the Shadow of Hitler*, 85–92; Heinrich A. Winkler, "Eternally in the Shadow of Hitler? The Dispute About the Germans' Understanding of History," in *Forever in the Shadow of Hitler*, 171–76.

20. Michael Stürmer, "How Much History Weighs," in *Forever in the Shadow of Hitler*, 196–97.

21. Eley, "Nazism," 180.

22. Michael Stürmer, "An Indictment that Fabricates Even Its Sources," in *Forever in the Shadow of Hitler*, 61–62.

23. Michael Stürmer, "History in a Land Without History," in *Forever in the Shadow of Hitler*, 16.

24. Strauss, cited in Eley, "Nazism," 194.

25. Kohl, cited in Eley, "Nazism," 194.

26. Habermas, "Settlement," 42.

27. Domansky, *"Kristallnacht,"* 74.

28. Brockmann, "Bitburg Deconstruction," 171.

29. Domansky, *"Kristallnacht,"* 71.

30. Timothy G. Ash, "Germany After Bitburg," in *Bitburg in Moral and Political Perspective*, ed. Geoffrey H. Hartmann (Bloomington: Indiana University Press, 1986), 199–203; Saul Friedländer, "Some German Struggles with Memory," in *Bitburg in Moral and Political Perspective*, 27–42; and Jürgen Habermas, "Defusing the Past: A Politico-Cultural Tract," in *Bitburg in Moral and Political Perspective*, 43–51.

31. Domansky, *"Kristallnacht,"* 75–76.

32. This "choice" was suggested by Habermas ("Defusing," 47).

33. Habermas, "Defusing," 49.

34. Friedländer, "Some German Struggles," 33.

35. Ash, "Germany After Bitburg," 200.

36. "Wir müssen die Maßstäbe allein finden. Schonung unserer Gefühle durch uns selbst oder durch andere hilft nicht weiter. Wir brauchen und wir haben die Kraft, der Wahrheit so gut wir es können ins Auge zu sehen, ohne Beschönigung und ohne Einseitigkeit. Der 8. Mai ist für uns vor allem ein Tag der Erinnerung an das, was Menschen erleiden mußten." All translations of Weizsäcker's speech are taken from Hartmann, *Bitburg in Moral and Political Perspective*, 262–73. The German text is from Girnth, *Einstellung*, 277–98.

37. "Wir gedenken heute in aller Trauer aller Toten des Krieges und der Gewaltherrschaft. Wir gedenken insbesondere der sechs Millionen Juden, die in deutschen Konzentrationslagern ermordet wurden. Wir gedenken aller Völker, die in Krieg gelitten haben, vor allem der unsäglich vielen Bürger der Sowjetunion und der Polen, die ihr Leben verloren haben. Als Deutschen gedenken wir in Trauer der eigenen Landsleute, die als Soldaten, bei den Fliegerangriffen in der Heimat . . . sterben mußten."

38. "Am Anfang der Gewaltherrschaft hatte der abgrundtiefe Haß Hitlers gegen unsere jüdischen Mitmenschen gestanden." "Die Ausführung der Verbrechen lag in der Hand weniger." "Es gab viele Formen, das Gewissen ablenken zu lassen, nicht zuständig zu sein, wegzuschauen, zu schweigen." "Jeder, der die Zeit mit vollem Bewußtsein erlebt hat, frage sich heute im stillen selbst nach seiner Verstrickung."

39. Weizsäcker's narrative account was the very one that Daniel Goldhagen transgressed with his book *Hitler's Willing Executioners: Ordinary Germans and the Holocaust* (New York: Alfred A. Knopf, 1996). The book, which met with a storm of protest by conservatives in Germany, argued that most Germans were involved in the Holocaust in one way or another. Construed as a "dramatically rejected" text, it too

would provide a useful site for the identification of strategies of remembrance in post-unification Germany.

40. "Der 8. Mai ist ein tiefer historischer Einschnitt, nicht nur in der deutschen, sondern auch in der europäischen Geschichte. Der europäische Bürgerkreig war an sein Ende gelangt, die alte europäische Welt zu Bruch gegangen." "Auf dem Weg in Unheil wurde Hitler die treibende Kraft. Er erzeugte und er nutzte Massenwahn. Eine schwache Demokratie war unfähig, ihm Einhalt zu gebieten. Und auch die europäische Westmächte, nach Churchills Urteil 'arglos, nicht schuldlos,' trugen durch Schwäche zur verhängnisvollen Entwicklung bei." " . . .wurde der deutsch-sowjetische Nichtangriffspakt geschlossen . . . um Hitler den Einmarsch in Polen zu ermöglichen. Das war der damaligen Führung der Sowjetunion voll bewußt. Allen politisch denkenden Menschen jener Zeit war klar, daß der deutsch-sowjetische Pakt Hitler Einmarsch in Polen und damit den Zweiten Weltkrieg bedeutete." "Dadurch wird die deutsche Schuld am Ausbruch des Zweiten Weltkrieges nicht verringert." This pattern of minimization followed by a blunted admission of responsibility was repeated throughout the address.

41. "[A]m Ende blieb nur noch ein Volk übrig, um gequält, geknechtet und geschändet zu werden; das eigene, das deutsche Volk."

42. ". . . wir selbst zu Opfern unseres eignen Krieges wurden." "In seiner Predigt zum 8. Mai sagte Kardinal Meißner in Ostberlin: 'Das trostlose Ergebnis der Sünde ist immer die Trennung.'"

43. "40 Jahre nach dem Ende des Krieges ist das deutsche Volk nach wie vor geteilt. . . . Wir Deutschen sind ein Volk und eine Nation. Wir fühlen uns zusammengehörig, weil wir dieselbe Geschichte durchlebt haben. Auch den 8. Mai 1945 haben wir als gemeinsames Schicksal unseres Volkes erlebt, das uns eint. . . . Die Menschen in Deutschland wollen gemeinsam einen Frieden, der Gerechtigkeit und Menschenrecht für alle Völker einschließt, auch für das unsrige. Nicht ein Europa der Mauern kann sich über Grenzen hinweg versöhnen, sondern ein Kontinent, der seinen Grenzen das Trennende nimmt."

44. Excerpts of the Jenninger speech are based on a comparison of three copies of the speech: Girnth, *Einstellung*, 251–76; a copy of the speech appearing in the November 25, 1988, issue of *Die Zeit*, No. 47; and an English translation of the speech obtained from the German Information Center in New York. All translations are ultimately my own.

45. "Bestürzender Mangel an Sensibilität," *Die Welt*, 11 November 1988, A5.

46. "Bundestag Deputies Protest Jenninger Remarks," *Foreign Bulletin Information Service*, WEU–88–220 (10 November 1988).

47. "Die Presse reagiert mit Empörung," *Die Welt*, 12 November 1988, E7.

48. Karl-Heinz Janßen, "Die Wahrheit nicht bezweifelt," *Die Zeit*, 18 November 1988, A3; Eghard Morbitz, "Eine ausgesprochen deutsche Tragödie," *Frankfurter Rundschau*, 12 November 1988, A3; and Roderich Reifenrath, "Warum mußte er reden?" *Frankfurter Rundschau*, 11 November 1988, A3.

49. Many West German critics readily noted that Jenninger's address was factually true. For example, see Christoph Bertram, "Ein würdiges Gedenker," *Die Zeit*, 18 November 1988, A5; and Günther Nonnenmacher, "Der Umgang mit unserer Geschichte," *Franfurter Allgemeine Zeitung*, 12 November 1988, A1.

50. Peter Polenz, "Verdünnte Sprachkulture: Das Jenninger-Syndrom in sprachkritischer Sicht," *Deutsche Sprache* 4 (1989): 289–316; Thomas B. Farrell, *Norms of Rhetorical Culture* (New Haven: Yale University Press, 1993), 308–21.

51. Farrell, *Norms of Rhetorical Culture*, 310.

52. Ibid., 312.

53. Ibid., 313.

54. Ibid., 316.

55. "Die Juden in Deutschland und in aller Welt gedenken heute der Ereignisse vor 50 Jahren. Auch wir Deutschen erinnern uns an das, was sich vor einem halben Jahrhundert in unserem Land zutrug. . . ."

56. Reifenrath, "Warum."

57. Heute nun haben wir uns im Deutschen Bundestag zusammengefunden, um hier im Parlament der Pogrome vom 9. und 10. November 1938 zu gedenken, weil nicht die Opfer, sondern wir, in deren Mitte die Verbrechen geschahen, erinnern und Rechenschaft ablegen müssen, weil wir Deutsche uns klarwerden wollen über das Verständnis unserer Geschichte und über Lehren für die politische Gestaltung unserer Gegenwart und Zukunft."

58. "Bei den Ausschreitungen handelte es sich nicht etwa um die Äußerungen eines wie immer motivierten spontanen Volkszorns, sondern um eine von der damaligen Staatsführung erdachte, angestiftete und geförderte Aktion."

59. "Nur wenige machten bei den Ausschreitungen mit. . . . Alle sahen, was geschah, aber die allermeisten schauten weg und schwiegen. Auch die Kirchen schwiegen."

60. "Mir wäre lieber gewesen, ihr hättet zweihundert Juden erschlagen und hättet nicht solche Werte vernichtet."

61. Several commentators noted that Jenninger's delivery so lacked vocal variety that it was impossible to distinguish when he was quoting someone from when he was speaking in his own voice. Walter Jens, "Ungehaltene Worte über eine gehalten Rede," *Die Zeit*, 18 November 1988, A3+; Helmut Herles, "Das mildeste Urteil lautet: Gut gemeint, aber nicht gekonnt," *Frankfurter Allgemeine Zeitung*, 11 November 1988, A3; Hans-Herbert Gäbel, "Kein Einzelfall," *Frankfurter Rundschau*, 12 November 1988, A3.

62. "Verdünnte Sprachkulture," 289–316. Polenz's focus is on style rather than content, whereas this study primarily focuses on content codes. Nevertheless, Polenz helpfully points out that stylistic expectations can also be transgressed.

63. Polenz, "Verdünnte Sprachkulture," 306.

64. "Im Rückblick wird deutlich . . . daß zwischen 1933 und 1938 tatsächlich eine Revolution in Deutschland stattfand—eine Revolution, in der sich der Rechsstaat in einen Unrechts- und Verbrechensstaat verwandelte."

65. "Hitlers sogenannte Weltanschauung fehlte jeder originäre Gedanke. Alles war schon vor him da: der zum biologistischen Rassismus gesteigerte Juden-haß ebenso wie der Affekt gegen die Moderne."

66. "Wir sind ohnmächtig angesichts dieser Sätze, wie wir ohnmächtig sind angesichts des millionenfachen Untergangs. Zahlen und Worte helfen nicht weiter. Das menschliche Leid ist nicht rückholbar; und jeder einzelne, der zum Opfer wurde, war für die Seinene unersetzlich. So bleibt ein Rest, an dem alle Versuche scheitern, zu erklären und zu begreifen."

67. "Selbstbefreiung in der Konfrontation mit dem Grauen ist weniger quälend als seine Verdrängung."

68. "Meine Damen und Herren, die Erinnerung wachzuhalten und die Vergangenheit als Teil unserer Identität als Deutsche anzunehmen—dies allein verheißt uns Älteren wie den Jüngeren Befreiung von der Last der Geschichte."

69. Kenneth Burke, "The Rhetoric of Hitler's Battle," in *Philosophy of Literary Form: Studies in Symbolic Action* (Berkeley: University of California Press, 1941), 340.

70. Stephen H. Browne, "Reading, Rhetoric, and the Texture of Public Memory," *Quarterly Journal of Speech* 81 (1995): 242.

## Chapter 3—The Discourse of Democracy in Post-Communist Russia

1. Gregory Gleason, "Nationalism and Its Discontents," *Russian Review* 53 (January 1993): 79–90; Iver B. Neumann, *Russia and the Idea of Europe: A Study in Identity and International Relations* (New York: Routledge, 1996); Liah Greenfield, "The Formation of the Russian National Identity: The Role of Status Insecurity and Ressentiment," *Comparative Studies in Society and History* 32 (1990): 549–91.

2. Thane Gustafson, *Capitalism Russian Style* (Cambridge: Cambridge University Press, 1999), 183.

3. Wedel, Janine R. *Collision and Collusion: The Strange Case of Western Aid to Eastern Europe* (New York: Palgrave, 2001); Anders Aslund, "Russia's Collapse," *Foreign Affairs* 78 (September/October 1999): 64–77; A. Frolov, "About the Real Subject of Market Reforms," *Russian Economic Journal* 1 (1999): 40–50; Vilan Perlamutrov, "Toward a Market Economy or Toward an Economic Catastrophe?" *Problems of Economic Transition* (1994): 24–40.

4. The following analysis will focus on democratic discourse that masked the triumph of a corrupt form of neoliberalism in Russia, not on the devastating material effects of those policies. For a discussion of the destruction wrought on average Russian citizens, see John Gray, *False Dawn* (New York: New Press, 1998), 133–65.

5. Richard Sakwa, *Russian Politics and Society* (New York: Routledge, 1993), 59; Maxim Boycko, Andrei Shleifer, and Robert Vishny, *Privatizing Russia* (Cambridge, Mass.: MIT Press, 1995); Michael Urban, "National Conflict Internalized: A Discourse

Analysis of the Fall of the First Russian Republic," in *The Myth of 'Ethnic Conflict': Politics, Economics, and 'Cultural Violence,'* ed. Beverly Crawford and Ronnie D. Lipschutz (Berkeley: University of California Press, 1998), 126–31.

6. John M. Goshko, "Yeltsin Receives Widespread Backing for Assault: In the U.S. Victory Seen for Democracy," *Washington Post*, 5 October 1993, A29.

7. Fred Kaplan, "Yeltsin Acts to Bolster His Powers," *Boston Globe*, 6 October 1993, A1.

8. "Yeltsin's Victory Seen as a Boost for Democracy," *Congressional Record*, 7 October 1993, A33.

9. Boris Yeltsin, "Yeltsin's Inaugural Address," *Dow Jones Interactive Library* (Online), Dow Jones News Retrieval, 10 July 1991.

10. Doyle McManus and Elizabeth Shogrun, "Yeltsin's Defiant Victory," *Los Angeles Times*, 22 August 1991, A1+.

11. Doyle McManus, "Clinton Messages His Support for Yeltsin," *Los Angeles Times*, 12 March 1993, A10.

12. While the 1993 legislative branch of government was elected, it was mostly composed of former Communist Party members, whom the pro-Yeltsin media referred to as "the Soviet *nomenklatura*."

13. William A. Clark, "Presidential Power and Democratic Stability Under the Russian Constitution: A Comparative Analysis," *Presidential Studies Quarterly* 28 (1998): 620.

14. Visiting Russia, I was in St. Petersburg in the days leading up to the election and was shocked and disappointed at the lack of vigorous election campaigning. Television reports focused almost exclusively on Putin in the course of his presidential duties (Yeltsin had basically turned the state over to Putin before the "election"), and large Putin campaign posters were in front of each subway stop. Across the entire city, one had to look hard for materials supporting other candidates.

15. Of course, the criteria for a *true* democracy are highly debatable. Judging democracy by the criteria of free elections and general freedom of speech and movement, Russia has obviously become a more democratic state. If, however, one also judges democracy, as many free trade economists and social philosophers do, by the additional criteria of effective rule of property and civil law, a strong and independent judiciary, a healthy civil society, and a well-regulated business environment (e.g., fair competition, general accounting standards, etc.), the Russian transition to democracy was far from complete when Putin assumed the presidency in 2000.

16. Paul A. Goble, "Three Faces of Nationalism in the Former Soviet Union," in *Nationalism and Nationalities in the New Europe*, ed. Charles A. Kupchan (Ithaca, N.Y.: Cornell University Press, 1995), 130. It should be noted that ethnic identity did play a role in collective identity construction among nonethnic Russians and that Russians recognized as ethnic Russians were the privileged class economically, politically, and socially, even in republics that were not historically "Russian."

17. Edward Walker, "Moscow and the Provinces: Economic and Political Dimensions of Russian Regionalism," *Eurasian Reports* 3 (1993): 56.

18. Ronald Grigor Suny, *The Revenge of the Past: Nationalism, Revolution, and the Collapse of the Soviet Union* (Stanford, Calif.: Stanford University Press, 1993), 112–13; Neumann, *Russia and the Idea of Europe*, 3–20; Gleason, "Nationalism and Its Discontents."

19. In 1989, 81.53 percent of the citizens of Russia were identified as ethnic Russians. The cultural variety of the imperial territories was even greater prior to and during the Soviet era (Sakwa, *Russian Politics and Society*, 176–77). Obviously many languages are spoken in Germany and Canada, but relatively speaking, the Russian Federation is more profoundly multilingual and multicultural.

20. Gleason, "Nationalism and Its Discontents," 81.

21. Richard Pipes, *The Formation of the Soviet Union* (Cambridge, Mass.: Harvard University Press, 1997), 6–7; Sakwa, *Russian Politics and Society*, 198–99; George Schöpflin, "National Identity in the Soviet Union and East Central Europe," *Ethnic and Racial Studies* 14 (1991): 7–12; Suny, *Revenge of the Past*, 23–30; Greenfield, *Nationalism*, 250–74; Neumann, *Russia and the Idea of Europe*, 28–35.

22. Michael Rywkin, *Moscow's Lost Empire* (New York: M. E. Sharpe, 1994), 138; David P. Calleo, "Reflections on the Idea of the Nation-State," in *Nationalism and Nationalities in the New Europe*, ed. Charles A. Kupchan (Ithaca: Cornell University Press, 1995), 31; Gleason, "Nationalism and Its Discontents," 82–83.

23. Goble, "Nationalism in the Former Soviet Union," 122–26; Pipes, *Formation of the Soviet Union*, 34–49. A sketch of nationalities policies from Marx to Yeltsin is provided by Rywkin, *Moscow's Lost Empire*, 159–93.

24. Cited in Rywkin, *Moscow's Lost Empire*, 161–62.

25. Rywkin, *Moscow's Lost Empire*, 162–63.

26. Ibid., 65–71.

27. More precisely, in 1993 there were 21 republics, 1 autonomous *oblast* (Birobijan), 10 autonomous *okrugs*, 49 administrative *oblasts*, 6 *krais*, and the cities of Moscow and St. Petersburg, for a total of 89 administrative areas (Sakwa, *Russian Politics and Society*, 36).

28. Robert Sharlet, "Russia's 'Ethnic' Republics and Constitutional Politics," *Eurasian Reports* 3 (1993): 43; Elizabeth Teague, "Center-Periphery Relations in the Russian Federation," in *National Identity and Ethnicity in Russia and the New States of Eurasia*, ed. Roman Szporluk (New York: M. E. Sharpe, 1994), 26.

29. Robert Sharlet, "Russian Constitutional Crisis: Law and Politics Under Yeltsin," *Post-Soviet Affairs* 9 (1993): 321.

30. Rywkin, *Moscow's Lost Empire*, 190.

31. Teague, "Center-Periphery," 30.

32. Gail W. Lapidus and Edward W. Walker, "Nationalism, Regionalism, and Federalism: Center-Periphery Relations in Post-Communist Russia," in *The New Russia: Troubled Transformation*, ed. Gail W. Lapidus (Boulder, Colo.: Westview, 1994), 83; Gleason, "Nationalism and Its Discontents," 79–80.

33. Sharlet, "Russia's 'Ethnic' Republics," 4.

34. Robert B. Ahdieh, *Russia's Constitutional Revolution: Legal Consciousness and the Transition to Democracy, 1985–1996* (University Park: Pennsylvania State University Press, 1997); Erik P. Hoffman, "Challenges to Viable Constitutionalism in Post-Soviet Russia," *Harriman Review* 7 (1994): 25; Robert Sharlet, "The New Russian Constitution and Its Political Impact," *Problems of Post-Communism* 42 (1995): 3–7.

35. Edward Walker, "The New Russian Constitution and the Future of the Russian Federation," *Harriman Institute Forum* 5 (1992): 10.

36. Ibid., 10.

37. Ibid.

38. Charles D. Tarlton, "Symmetry and Asymmetry as Elements of Federalism: A Theoretical Speculation," *Journal of Politics* 27 (1965): 861–74.

39. There were many constitutional drafts from a variety of sources, but these three arguably played the greatest role in the public debates.

40. The Supreme Soviet was a regularly meeting committee of the larger Congress of People's Deputies and was empowered to set the agenda of the Congress and to make decisions on its behalf.

41. Yitzhak M. Brudny, "Ruslan Khasbulatov, Aleksandr Rutskoi, and Intra-elite Conflict in Post-Communist Russia: 1991–1994," in *Patterns of Post-Soviet Leadership*, ed. Timothy J. Colton and Robert C. Tucker (Boulder, Colo.: Westview Press, 1995), 90. The effects of market reforms were especially problematic for many of the massive and geographically dispersed Soviet company towns built up around monolithic industries.

42. Vera Tolz, "Power Struggle in Russia: The Role of the Republics and Regions," *RFE/RL Research Report*, 9 April 1993, 10.

43. Ibid., 11–12.

44. Urban, "National Conflict," 112–27.

45. Ibid., 123.

46. Richard D. Anderson Jr., Valeri I. Chervyakov, and Pavel B. Parshin, "Words Matter: Linguistic Conditions for Democracy in Russia," *Slavic Review* (1995): 1–12.

47. Sakwa, *Russian Politics and Society*, 125.

48. Brudny, "Ruslan," 91–92.

49. Boris Yeltsin, *The Struggle for Russia*, trans. Catherine A. Fitzpatrick (New York: Belka, 1994), 205.

50. Ibid., 205.

51. All quotations from Yeltsin's address are taken from the English translation provided by the Official Kremlin International News Broadcast (20 March 1993). The translation was compared with videotaped excerpts of the speech with the aid of Russian translator Masha Sharikova of the Davis Center for Russian Studies at Harvard University. Ms. Sharikova also provided translations of all accounts in the Russian media.

52. For a discussion of dissociation as a form of argument, see Chaim Perelman, *The Realm of Rhetoric* (Notre Dame: University of Notre Dame Press, 1969), 126–37.

53. Sakwa, *Russian Politics and Society*, 7.

54. Yeltsin believed that this had been a set-up, for he claims to have shared the draft with Rutskoi and Zorkin in advance of his address (see Yeltsin, *Struggle for Russia*, 206–7).

55. Nikolau Pavlov, "Yeltsin's Fiasco—A Slap on the Cheek—On the Results of the Eighth Congress of the People's Deputies of Russia," *Den'*, 21–28 March 1993, 1.

56. Ibid.

57. Vitaly Tretyakov, "Don't Make Any More Mistakes," *Nezavisimaia Gazeta*, 23 March 1993, 1.

58. Valentin Tolstyh, editorial, *Nezavisimaia Gazeta*, 23 March 1993, 3.

59. "Obraschenie presidenta RF k grazhdanam rossii I otvet emu chitatelei pravdy," *Pravda*, 24 March 1993, 1+.

60. Yeltsin, *Struggle for Russia*, 207.

61. Ibid.

62. John M. Broder, "Clinton Stresses Yeltsin Support," *Los Angeles Times*, 24 March 1993, A1+.

63. Ibid.

64. "Statement by the Russian Government," *Izvestia*, 23 March 1993, 1.

65. Andrey Kolesnikova, *Rossijskie Vestie*, 24 March 1993, 1.

66. Boris Grushin, *Rossijskie Vestie*, 24 March 1993, 1.

67. Sharlet, "Russia's 'Ethnic' Republics," 4.

68. Yeltsin, *Struggle for Russia*, 212.

69. Sharlet, "The Prospects for Federalism in Russian Constitutional Politics," *Publius* 24, 2 (1994): 120.

70. Sakwa, *Russian Politics and Society*, 57; Yeltsin, *Struggle for Russia*, 209–15.

71. Brudny, "Ruslan," 82.

72. Sakwa, *Russian Politics and Society*, 57.

73. Ibid., 58.

74. Boris Yeltsin, "Opening Speech to the Constitutional Assembly," *BBC Summary of World Broadcasts*, 7 June 1993, 63–71. For comparative purposes, the Russian text of the address from *Konstitutsionnoe Soveshchanie*, August 1993, 22–20, was consulted. All excerpts are taken from the *BBC Summary* unless otherwise noted.

75. Teague, "Center-Periphery," 44; Sharlet, *Russian Politics and Society*, 4.

76. Olga Garvuzova, "Kommunopatrioty Zhdali Khasbulatova," *Nezavisimaia Gazeta*, 6 June 1993, 2.

77. Olivia Ward, "Russian Talks on Constitution Off to Rocky Start," *Toronto Star*, 6 June 1993, A2; Vera Tolz, "Drafting the New Russian Constitution," *RFE/RL Research Report* 2, 29 (1993): 9.

78. A similar strategy could be seen in West Germany, where the National Socialist period was characterized as a deviation from the otherwise "democratic" tendencies in Germany.

79. Despite Yeltsin's promises, however, no such Treaty was included in the new Russian constitution. Sakwa, *Russian Politics and Society*, 187; Lapidus and Walker, "Nationalism," 93.

80. Yeltsin, "Opening Speech," 63. Page references in the following paragraphs are to the English text in the *BBC Summary* (see above, n. 75).

81. Sergei Alekseev, "Vystuplenie predsedatelya Soveta Issledovatelskogo tsentra chastnogo praca pri presidente," *Rossijskie Vestie*, 8 June 1993, 3.

82. Ruslan Khasbulatov, "Verkhovnyi Sovet—Za Konstruktivnoe Sotrudnichestvo," *Rossiskaia Gazeta*, 8 June 1993, 1+.

83. "'Radio Parliament' Rallies to the Defence of Khasbulatov," *BBC Summary of World Broadcasts*, 9 June 1993; "Obrashchenie K Grazhdanam Rossiiskoi Federatsii," *Pravda*, 8 June 1993, 1.

84. Aleksandr Linkov, "Uidet Predstavitelnaia Vlast—Pridet Diktatura," *Rossiskaia Gazeta*, 8 June 1993, 2.

85. Viktor Sapov, "Demokratiia Pod Bashmakom Prezidenta. V. Chechne—Pod Gusenitsami Tankov," *Pravda*, 8 June 1993, 1+.

86. Ibid.

87. Ibid.

88. "Address to the Citizens of the Russian Federation," *Pravda*, 8 June 1993, 1.

89. Victor Trushkov, editorial, *Pravda*, 8 June 1993, 1.

90. Lapidus and Walker, "Center-Periphery," 99.

91. T. H. Rigby, "Conclusion: Russia in Search of Its Future," in *Russia in Search of its Future*, ed. Amin Saikal and William Maley (Cambridge: Cambridge University Press, 1995), 220.

92. Brudny, "Ruslan," 94; Sakwa, *Russian Politics and Society*, 127.

93. Ahdieh, *Russia's Constitutional Revolution*, 65.

94. Ibid., 66; Boris Yeltsin, "On the Step by Step Constitutional Reform of the Russian Federation," *Dow Jones Interactive Library* (Online), *Dow Jones News Retrieval*, 21 September 1993. The address was compared with videotaped portions of the address and excerpts that appeared in *Current Digest of the Post-Soviet Press* 45, 38 (1993): 1.

95. Ruslan Khasbulatov, "The President Is Trampling on the Constitution: In the Hour of Trial, Rise to the Defense of Democracy," *Rossiskaia Gazeta*, 23 September 1993, 1+.

96. "Parliament Ousts Yeltsin, Names Rutskoi President," *Current Digest of the Post-Soviet Press*, 45, 38 (1993): 4–5.

97. Ahdieh, *Russia's Constitutional Revolution*, 66; Kaplan, "Yeltsin Acts."

98. Robert C. Tucker, "Post-Soviet Leadership and Change," in *Patterns in Post-Soviet Leadership*, ed. Timothy J. Colton and Robert C. Tucker (Boulder, Colo.: Westview Press, 1995), 22.

99. Lilia Shevtsova, "Russia's Post-Communist Politics: Revolution or Continuity," in *The New Russia: Troubled Transformation*, ed. Gail W. Lapidus (Boulder, Colo.: Westview Press, 1995), 22–23; Kaplan, "Yeltsin Acts."

100. Goshko, "Yeltsin Receives Widespread Backing."

101. Leonid Nikitinskii, "We Still Have a Choice Between Two Democracies," *Izvestia*, 23 September 1993, 3; Nikolai Sakharov, "The President Must Have a Right to Dissolve the Parliament," *Rossiskaia Gazeta*, 23 September 1993, 2.

102. Kaplan, "Yeltsin Acts."

103. Hoffman, "Challenges to Viable Constitutionalism," 46. For an extensive discussion of the shortcomings of the new constitution, see Ahdieh, Russia's *Constitutional Revolution*, 64–78. Eugene Huskey, "Democracy and Institutional Design in Russia," *Demokratizatsiya: The Journal of Post-Soviet Democratization* 4 (1996): 461–65.

104. Hoffman, "Challenges to Viable Constitutionalism," 37–43; Steven M. Miner, "Yeltsin Is Democrat Enough for His Times," *Newsday*, 7 October 1993, 127; George Rodriguez, "Empty Victory," *Fort Lauderdale Sun Sentinel*, 10 October 1993, G1; Robert Scheer, "Giving Yeltsin a Blank Check Is Disastrous," *Los Angeles Times*, 5 November 1993, B7; Dimitri Simes, "Testing Yeltsin's Authoritarian Reflexes," *Washington Post*, 6 October 1991, C1; Jonathan Steele, "The President Who Would Become Tsar," *London Guardian*, 3 June 1993, 9.

105. James Hughes, "Regionalism in Russia: The Rise and Fall of the Siberian Agreement," *Europe-Asia Studies* 46, 7 (1994): 1153.

106. Ibid.

107. Hoffman, "Challenges to Viable Constitutionalism," 40.

108. Simes, "Testing."

109. Walker, "The New Russian Constitution," 11.

110. Shevtsova, "Russia's Post-Communist Politics," 17.

111. Ibid., 25.

112. Huskey, "Democracy," 461.

113. David Lempert, "Changing Russian Political Culture in the 1990s: Parasites, Paradigms, and Perestroika," *Comparative Studies in Society and History* 35 (1993): 640.

114. Sakwa, *Russian Politics and Society*, 171.

115. John Dunn, *Western Political Theory in the Face of the Future* (New York: Cambridge University Press, 1979), 12.

116. Ernest Laclau and Chantal Mouffe, *Hegemony and Socialist Strategy: Towards a Radical Democratic Politics* (New York: Verso, 1985). The entire book is an argument for a discursive politics in which subjects consistently critique the narrative absences that their identities require ad infinitum.

117. The paradox does not escape me that, in an argument about different political forces using democratic discourse to characterize a wide variety of political agendas, I have my own characterization. Democracy as the institutionalized critique of power/hegemony is, however, consistent with the democratic theory of Laclau and Mouffe.

118. In *False Dawn*, Gray describes the situation in Russia as "anarcho-capitalism," and the general lawlessness of contemporary Russia is widely recognized.

119. For a discussion of the criteria for a "viable constitution" and the shortcomings of the new Russian constitution, see Hoffman, "Challenges to Viable Constitutionalism."

120. McManus, "Clinton Messages His Support."

121. Goshko, "Yeltsin Receives Widespread Backing."

122. Ibid.

123. Anyone who doubts that Russia has become a criminalized state need only look at the statistics. According to the numbers provided by Russia's Ministry of Internal

Affairs, in 1998 more than 40 percent of enterprise groups and 60 percent of banks were under the control of criminals, and between 1991 and 1995 known criminal groups grew from 952 to 8,222. The Ministry projects that these numbers doubled between 1995 and 2000. See N. Lapina and A. Chirikova, "Regionalnye ekonomicheskiye eilty: Mentalitet, povedenie, vzaimodeystviye so vlastiuy," *Obschevestvo I edonomika* 6 (1999): 277.

124. Kaplan, "Yeltsin Acts."

125. A unique combination of corporate welfare, industrial espionage on the part of Western consultants, and the criminalization of the privatization program were ultimately at the heart of the failures of "democratic" reform. For those interested in the details and in the part played by Harvard University and the United States Department of the Treasury, see Wedel (2001). Harvard professors in charge of the privatization program were later indicted for fraud and conspiracy (see Robbins et al., "U.S. Plans to File Suit Against Harvard Over Its Russian Foreign Aid Program," Wall Street Journal, 26 September 2000, A-4). Sakwa, *Russian Politics and Society*, 172.

126. Aslund, "Russia's Collapse," 65–66.

127. William E. Scheuerman, "Globalization and Exceptional Powers: The Erosion of Liberal Democracy," *Radical Philosophy* 93 (1999): 14–15.

128. David Lempert, "Changing Russian Political Culture," 642.

129. Ibid., 644.

### Chapter 4—Shifting Strategies of Remembrance in Quebec

1. Dan Lett and Doug Nairne, "Bouchard Vows Quick Return, Parizeau Stuns," *Winnipeg Free Press*, 31 October 1995, A1+.

2. Doug Nairn, "Dream Dies, Crowd Weeps," *Winnipeg Free Press*, 31 October 1995, A1+.

3. Donald McKenzie, "Numerically Speaking, Parizeau May Be Right: Ethnic Vote Pro-No, But Premier's Swipe a No-No," *Winnipeg Free Press*, 1 November 1995, B2. Almost every region outside Montreal voted to secede, as did 60 percent of Quebec's francophone population, but allophones and anglophones in the province voted 95 percent No (Michele Ouimet, "Les Francophones ont aussie aidé le NON," *La Presse*, 1 November 1995, B8). All French translations are by Professor Barbara Warnick, University of Washington. The term *francophone* refers to an individual for whom French is their first language. *Anglophone* refers to English speakers, while *allophone* refers to those whose primary language is neither French nor English.

4. Cristina S. Blanc, Linda Basch, and Nina Glick Schiller, "Transnationalism, Nation-States, and Culture," *Current Anthropology* 16 (1995): 683–86.

5. Ernest Gellner, *Nations and Nationalism* (Oxford: Basil Blackwell, 1983), 36–38.

6. Paul R. Brass, "Elite Competition and Nation-Formation," in *Nationalism*, ed. John Hutchinson and Anthony D. Smith (New York: Oxford University Press, 1994), 87.

7. Cornel West, "A Matter of Life and Death," in *The Identity In Question*, ed. John Rajchman (New York: Routledge, 1995), 17.

8. Immanual Wallerstein, "Class Conflict in the Capitalist World-Economy," in *Race, Nation, Class: Ambiguous Identities* (New York: Verso, 1991), 122.

9. Claude Gamache, "Two Visions: The Canadian Dilemma," *Winnipeg Free Press*, 30 October 1995, A7; Gilles Gougeon, *A History of Québec Nationalism*, trans. Louisa Blair, Robert Chodos, and Jane Ubertino (Toronto: James Lorimer & Company, 1994); Richard Handler, *Nationalism and the Politics of Culture in Québec* (Madison: University of Wisconsin Press, 1988).

10. Will Kymlicka, "Social Unity in a Liberal State," in *The Communitarian Challenge to Liberalism*, ed. Ellen F. Paul, Fred D. Miller Jr., and Jeffrey Paul (Cambridge: Cambridge University Press, 1996), 105–36.

11. Gregory Jusdanis, "Beyond National Culture?" *Boundary 2* 22 (1995): 23–60.

12. Christian Dufour, *A Canadian Challenge* (Lantzville, B.C.: Oolichan Books, 1990); Gougeon, *History of Québec Nationalism*; Camille Legendre, *French Canada in Crisis: A New Society in the Making?* (London: Expedite Graphic Limited, 1980); Marcel Rioux, "The Development of Ideologies in Quebec," in *A Passion for Identity*, ed. Eli Mandel and David Taras (Agincourt, Ont.: Methuen, 1987), 267–88.

13. Dufour, *Canadian Challenge*, 17–18. This reading is particularly notable in the "monumental" historiography of Lionel Groulx as well as historians of the 1960s and 1970s inspired by the work of Franz Fanon.

14. Robert Lahaise, "Interview with Robert Lahaise," in Gougeon, *A History of Québec Nationalism*, 4–16.

15. Fears of colonial subjugation certainly do not completely dominate the national imaginary of French Canadians. They have not usually been separatists, but dedicated federalists fighting for political supremacy in the legislature. The Rebellions of 1837–38, for example, were not separatist but populist and republican. French Canadians have consistently played major roles in federal politics; and Georges-Etienne Cartier, Wilfred Laurier, Pierre Trudeau, and Jean Chrétien have all been staunch federalists. Still, despite the problematic nature of "colonial" narratives, ethnic and cultural forms of national identity have drawn upon such narratives in public arguments for Quebec sovereignty.

16. Jean-Paul Bernard, "Interview with Jean-Paul Bernard," in Gougeon, *History of Québec Nationalism*, 19.

17. Cited in Rioux, "Development of Ideologies," 269–70. Arguably, the more recent history of Canada has refuted Lord Durham's assertion.

18. Legendre, *French Canada in Crisis*, 9.

19. Dufour, *A Canadian Challenge*, 91.

20. Handler, *Nationalism and the Politics of Culture*, discusses this process at length.

21. For a very useful discussion of Canadian identity wars related to the construction of the new constitution, see Colin H. Williams, "A Requiem for Canada," *Federalism: The Multiethnic Culture*, ed. Graham Smith (New York: Longman, 1995), 31–72.

22. Biographical information on Parizeau and Bouchard was taken from the *Parti Québécois* home page, http://198.168.84.30/en/gens/chefs (11 July 1996).

23. Excerpts from the following speeches are English translations provided on the *Parti Québécois* homepage, http://198.168.84.30/en/idees/disc (11 July 1996).

24. While strategies of remembrance are most easily identified through the analysis of failed speech, speech that succeeds or is relatively uncontroversial (as we saw with Weizsäcker's address in West Germany) is nevertheless useful to critics of public memory. Parizeau's later dramatic failure confirms that economic strategies were far superior to ethnic strategies for those seeking to maximize federal power for, and citizen allegiance to, Quebec.

25. Etienne Balibar and Immanuel Wallerstein, *Race, Nation, Class: Ambiguous Identities*, trans. Chris Turner (Verso: New York, 1991), 59–60.

26. Tu Thanh Ha, "Yes Vote No Picnic, Chrétien Warns," *Globe and Mail*, 19 October 1995, A1+; Marian Stinson, "Dollar Plunges on Fears of Yes Vote," *Globe and Mail*, 21 October 1995, A1+; Alan Freeman, "Document Outlines Steps Against Sovereignty," *Globe and Mail*, 21 October 1995, A1+.

27. As in Germany, historians also wanted to play a role in pan-Canadian national identity construction. For example, Michael Bliss, history professor at the University of Toronto, observed that Canadians were "immersed in the most intense debate about [their] future as a people since Confederation" and that there was a "hunger" on the part of Canadians "for help in understanding where we came from, who we are, and where we might be going" and that "we have a duty as scholars, university teachers, and citizens to do all that we can to meet that demand" ("Privatizing the Mind: The Sundering of Canadian History, the Sundering of Canada," *Journal of Canadian Studies* 26 [1992]: 6–11).

28. In many ways, Lord Durham's recommendations were not those taken seriously in constitutional arrangements. The terms of the Treaty of Paris, the Quebec Act of 1774, the Constitution Act of 1791, and even the Constitution Act of 1982 can all be read as providing concrete political and cultural guarantees to French Canadian citizens.

29. William D. Coleman, "From Bill 22 to Bill 101: The Politics of Language Under the *Parti Québécois*," *Canadian Journal of Political Science* 14 (1981): 459–85.

30. Dufour, *A Canadian Challenge*, 129.

31. This divergence of the national imaginary in Canada at the time was outlined by secessionist supporter Guy Laforest and former Canadian Prime Minister Pierre Trudeau. LaForest's basic argument was that the federalist tendency represented English Canadian interests at the expense of French Canadian language and culture, and that recent constitutional reform had been designed according to the English colonial spirit of conquest. Conversely, Trudeau argued that Quebec secessionists had already won language and cultural protection from those same constitutional reforms, and that arguments of ethnic protectionism were merely a smokescreen for maximizing economic and political power within the federation.

32. Pierre E. Trudeau, *Pierre Trudeau Speaks Out on Meech Lake* (Toronto: General Paperbacks, 1990), 46. During constitutional battles after the American Revolution, a similar argument was made against the clause in the Articles of Confederation requiring unanimous consent.

33. Ibid., 54.

34. Ibid., 46.

35. Ibid., 61. It was the "notwithstanding clause" that allowed the *Parti Québécois* to pass its francophone legislation contradicting federal bilingualism.

36. Guy LaForest, "Fraud, Shame and Injustice," *Globe and Mail*, 30 October 1995, A21.

37. Charles Taylor, *Multiculturalism: Examining the Politics of Recognition*, ed. Amy Gutman (Princeton, N.J.: Princeton University Press, 1994), 54–61.

38. According to Statistics Canada, in 1991 Quebec was populated by approximately 27 million Catholics and 15 million non-Catholics, with the French language roughly following along those same lines (http://www.statcan.ca/english/pgbd/people/population/demo30b.htm [1 June 2001]).

39. As Balibar and Wallerstein have noted, there is an intimate relationship between certain forms of nationalism and racism, especially if racism is conceptualized as over-identification with a noncivic identity (*Race, Nation, Class*, 48–49).

40. Ibid., 59–60.

41. Asselin Charles, "Why Immigrants and Minorities Feel Discomfort in Quebec," *Globe and Mail*, 17 October 1995, A19.

42. Richard Mackie, "Yes 50.2, No 49.8, Poll Suggests: Emotional Factors Affect Voters' Decisions as Bouchard's Speeches Galvanize Yes Campaign," *Globe and Mail*, 21 October 1995, A1+; Richard Mackie, "Bouchard Berated at Rally of 3,000 Federalist Women," *Globe and Mail*, 28 October 1995, A3.

43. Tu Thanh Ha, "Bouchard Remarks Spark Outcry: Yes Leader Dismisses Attacks Over 'White Races' Comment as Petty Politicking," *Globe and Mail*, 16 October 1995, A1+.

44. Tu Thanh Ha, "Bouchard Defends 'White Race' Remark," *Globe and Mail*, 17 October 1995, A1+.

45. Tu Thanh Ha, "Bouchard Comment Puzzling," *Globe and Mail*, 17 October 1995, A18.

46. Ha, "Bouchard Remarks."

47. Charles, "Why Immigrants."

48. "Mr. Bouchard's Ethnic Nationalism," *Globe and Mail*, 17 October 1995, A18.

49. Denis Lessard, "Lucien Bouchard S'en Vient," *La Presse*, 1 November 1995, A1+.

50. Parizeau's speech, as well as the reporters' comments that followed, was broadcast on October 30, 1995. English translations provided by the CBC.

51. Lessard, "Lucien Bouchard."

52. Lysiane Gagnon, "Triste fin de carrière," *La Presse*, 1 November 1995, B3.

53. McKenzie, "Numerically Speaking."

54. Lucien Bouchard, "Quebeckers Must Not Forget How to Live Together," *Canadian Speeches* 9 (1996): 20–28.

55. Ibid., 21.

56. Ibid., 25.

57. Taylor, *Multiculturalism*, 43.

58. Masao Miyoshi, "A Borderless World? From Colonialism to Transnationalism and the Decline of the Nation-State," *Critical Inquiry* 19 (1993): 726–51. Chandran Kukathas and Graham Smith engage in useful discussions about the differences between liberalism and communitarianism. Basically, liberal political philosophy holds that individual rights always take priority over collective rights, and that the laws/procedures, not the aims, of societies should be regulated by the state. Communitarian political philosophy holds that collective rights may at times take priority over individual rights, since collective aims, as well as laws/procedures, are concerns of the state. See Chandran Kukathas, "Liberalism, Communitarianism, and Political Community," in *The Communitarian Challenge to Liberalism*, ed. Ellen F. Paul, Fred D. Miller, and Jeffrey Paul (Cambridge: Cambridge University Press, 1996), 80–104; and Graham Smith, "Mapping the Federal Condition: Ideology, Political Practice and Social Justice," in *Federalism: The Multiethnic Challenge*, ed. Graham Smith (New York: Longman, 1995), 1–28. Federal characterizations of Canadian identity generally followed liberal theories, while those in Quebec generally followed communitarian theories.

## Chapter 5 — Strategic Memory, National Identity, World Order

1. Iver B. Neumann, *Russia and the Idea of Europe* (New York: Routledge, 1996), 100.

2. For a discussion of national identity as imagined, see Benedict Anderson, *Imagined Communities* (New York: Verso, 1983).

3. Frederick M. Dolan, *Allegories of America* (Ithaca, N.Y.: Cornell University Press, 1994), 168.

4. Ernst Cassirer, *The Myth of the State* (New Haven, Conn.: Yale University Press, 1946).

5. Chantal Mouffe, "Democratic Politics and the Question of Identity," in *The Identity in Question*, ed. John Rajchman (New York: Routledge, 1995), 36.

6. Ibid., 42.

7. Following Foucault's formulation, I assume that power is relational. See Michel Foucault, "The Subject and Power," Afterword to *Michel Foucault: Beyond Structuralism and Hermeneutics*, ed. Hubert Dreyfus and Paul Rabinow (Brighton: Harvester Press, 1982). Knowledge has no necessary relation to Truth, but wherever the Truth is thought to reside, there also resides relational power. Cultural nationalism particularly tends to create a sense of Truth in socially constructed subjects. In this study, German historians, Russian Eurasianists, and conservative clerical nationalists in Quebec each argued that their respective "nations" were on a "special path" or had a unique "spiritual mission."

NOTES TO PAGES 90–100 — 123

8. Anthony D. Smith, *National Identity* (Las Vegas: University of Nevada Press, 1991), 20.

9. Ibid., 20. This distinction is popularly known in the literature on national identity as the debate between "primordialists" and "instrumentalists."

10. Neumann, *Russia and the Idea of Europe*, 99.

11. Ibid., 86.

12. Smith, *National Identity*, 18.

13. Ibid., 8–15.

14. Jean Baudrillard, *For a Critique of the Political Economy of the Sign*, trans. Charles Levin (St. Louis, Mo.: Telos Press, 1981).

15. Etienne Balibar and Immanuel Wallerstein, *Race, Nation, Class: Ambiguous Identities*, trans. Chris Turner (New York: Verso, 1991); Miyoshi, "A Borderless World?" *Critical Inquiry* 19 (summer 1993): 726–51. Recent attempts at creating "global constitutions" for trade and finance, such as the 1997 Multilateral Agreement on Investment, raise additional doubts about the democratic pretensions of "liberal" constitutions.

16. Honi Fern Haber, *Beyond Postmodern Politics* (New York: Routledge, 1994), 131.

17. Kenneth Burke, "The Rhetoric of Hitler's Battle," in *Philosophy of Literary Form: Studies in Symbolic Action* (Baton Rouge: Louisiana State University Press, 1966), 330; italics in original.

18. Ibid., 340.

# BIBLIOGRAPHY

"Address to the Citizens of the Russia Federation." *Pravda*, 8 June 1993, 1.

Ahdieh, Robert B. *Russia's Constitutional Revolution: Legal Consciousness and the Transition to Democracy 1985–1996*. University Park: Pennsylvania State University Press, 1997.

Alekseev, Sergie. "Vystuplenie predsedatelya Soveta Issledovatelskogo tsentra chastnogo praca pri presidente." *Rossijskie Vestie*, 8 June 1993, 3.

Althusser, Louis. "Ideology and Ideological State Apparatuses." *Critical Theory Since 1965*. Edited by Hazard Adams and Leroy Searle. Tallahassee: Florida State University Press, 1986.

Anderson, Benedict. *Imagined Communities*. New York: Verso, 1983.

Anderson, Richard D. Jr., Valeri I. Chervyakov, Pavel B. Parshin. "Words Matter: Linguistic Conditions for Democracy in Russia." *Slavic Review* (1995): 1–12.

Ash, Timothy Garton. "Germany After Bitburg." In *Bitburg in Moral and Political Perspective*, edited by Geoffrey H. Hartman, 199–203. Bloomington: Indiana University Press, 1986.

Aslund, Anders. "Russia's Collapse." *Foreign Affairs* 78 (1999): 64–77.

Baldwin, Peter, ed. *Reworking the Past: Hitler, the Holocaust and the Historian's Debate*. Boston: Beacon Press, 1990.

Balibar, Etienne, and Immanuel Wallerstein. *Race, Nation, Class: Ambiguous Identities*. Translated by Chris Turner. New York: Verso, 1991.

Baudrillard, Jean. *For a Critique of the Political Economy of the Sign*. Translated by Charles Levin. St. Louis, Mo.: Telos Press, 1981.

Berger, Stefan. "Historians and Nation-Building in Germany after Reunification." *Past and Present* 148 (1995): 187–222.

Bernard, Jean-Paul. "Interview with Jean-Paul Bernard." In Gilles Gougeon, ed., *A History of Québec Nationalism*, translated by Louisa Blair, Robert Chodos, and Jane Ubertino, 17–26. Toronto: James Lorimer & Company, 1994.

Bertram, Christoph. "Ein würdiges Gedenker." *Die Zeit*, 18 November 1988, A5.

"Bestürzender Mangel an Sensibilität." *Die Welt*, 11 November 1988, A5.

Billig, Michael. *Banal Nationalism*. Thousand Oaks, Calif.: Sage, 1995.

Blair, Carol, Marsha Jeppeson, and Enrico Pucci Jr. "Public Memorialization in Postmodernity: The Vietnam Veterans Memorial as Prototype." *Quarterly Journal of Speech* 77 (1991): 263–88.

Blanc, Cristina S., Linda Basch, and Nina Glick Schiller. "Transnationalism, Nation-States, and Culture." *Current Anthropology* 16 (1995): 683–86.

Bloom, William. *Personal Identity, National Identity, and International Relations*. Cambridge: Cambridge University Press, 1990.

Bliss, Michael. "Privatizing the Mind: The Sundering of Canadian History, the Sundering of Canada." *Journal of Canadian Studies* 26 (1992): 6–11.

Bouchard, Lucien. "Quebeckers Must Not Forget How to Live Together." *Canadian Speeches* 9 (1996): 20–28.

Boycko, Maxim, Andrei Shleifer, and Robert Vishny. *Privatizing Russia.* Cambridge, Mass.: MIT Press, 1995.

Brass, Paul R. "Elite Competition and Nation-Formation." In *Nationalism,* edited by John Hutchinson and Anthony D. Smith. New York: Oxford University Press, 1994.

Breuilly, John. *Nationalism and the State,* 2d ed. Chicago: University of Chicago Press, 1993.

Brockmann, Stephen. "Bitburg Deconstruction." *Philosophical Forum* 17 (1986): 159–74.

Broder, John M. "Clinton Stresses Yeltsin Support." *Los Angeles Times,* 24 March 1993, A1+.

Broszat, Martin. "A Plea for the Historicization of National Socialism." In *Reworking the Past: Hitler, the Holocaust, and the Historian's Debate,* edited by Peter Baldwin, 77–87. Boston: Beacon Press, 1990.

Browne, Stephen H. "Reading, Rhetoric, and the Texture of Public Memory. *Quarterly Journal of Speech* 81 (1995): 237–50.

Brudny, Yitzhak M. "Ruslan Khasbulatov, Aleksandr Rutskoi, and Intra-elite Conflict in Post-Communist Russia: 1991–1994." In *Patterns of Post-Soviet Leadership,* edited by Timothy J. Colton and Robert C. Tucker, 75–102. Boulder, Colo.: Westview Press, 1995.

"Bundestag Deputies Protest Jenninger Remarks." *Foreign Bulletin Information Service* (WEU-88-220), 10 November 1988.

Burke, Kenneth. "The Rhetoric of Hitler's 'Battle.'" *Philosophy of Literary Form: Studies in Symbolic Action.* Baton Rouge: Louisiana State University Press, 1941.

Büsch, Otto, and James J. Sheehan, eds. *Die Rolle der Nation in der deutschen Geschichte und Gegenwart.* Berlin: Colloquium Verlag, 1985.

Butler, Judith. *Gender Trouble: Feminism and the Subversion of Identity.* New York: Routledge, 1990.

Calhoun, Craig. *Nationalism.* Minneapolis: University of Minnesota Press, 1997.

Calleo, David P. "Reflections on the Idea of the Nation-State." *Nationalism and Nationalities in the New Europe,* edited by Charles A. Kupchan, 15–36. Ithaca: Cornell University Press, 1995, 15–36.

Carruthers, Bruce G. *City of Capital: Politics and Markets in the English Financial Revolution.* Princeton, N.J.: Princeton University Press, 1996.

Cassirer, Ernst. *The Myth of the State.* New Haven, Conn.: Yale University Press, 1946.

Charland, Maurice. "Constitutive Rhetoric: The Case of the Peuple Québécois." *Quarterly Journal of Speech* 73 (1987): 133–50.

Charles, Asselin. "Why Immigrants and Minorities Feel Discomfort in Québec." *Globe and Mail,* 17 October 1995, A19.

Clark, William A. "Presidential Power and Democratic Stability Under the Russian Constitution: A Comparative Analysis." *Presidential Studies Quarterly* 28 (1998): 620–37.

Coleman, William D. "From Bill 22 to Bill 101: The Politics of Language under the Parti Québécois." *Canadian Journal of Political Science* 14 (1981): 459–85.

Connor, Walker. "Nation-Building or Nation-Destroying," *World Politics* 24 (1972): 319–55.

Connolly, William S. *Identity/Difference: Democratic Negotiations of Political Paradox.* Ithaca, N.Y.: Cornell University Press, 1991.

Cox, Robert J. "Memory, Critical Theory, and the Argument from History." *Argumentation and Advocacy* 27 (1990): 1–13.

"Die Presse reagiert mit Empörung." *Die Welt,* 12 November 1988, E7.

Dolan, Frederick M. *Allegories of America.* Ithaca, N.Y.: Cornell University Press, 1994.

Domansky, Elizabeth. "'Kristallnacht,' the Holocaust and German Unity: The Meaning of November 9 as an Anniversary in Germany." *History & Memory* 4 (1992): 60–94.

Dreyfus, H. L., and P. Rabinow, eds. *Michel Foucault: Beyond Structuralism and Hermeneutics.* Chicago: University of Chicago Press, 1983.

Dufour, Christian. *A Canadian Challenge.* Lantzville, B.C.: Oolichan Books, 1990.

Dunn, John. *Western Political Theory in the Face of the Future.* New York: Cambridge University Press, 1979.

Eley, Geoff. "Nazism, Politics and Public Memory: Thoughts on the West German *Historikerstreit* 1986–1987." *Past & Present* 121 (1988): 171–208.

Farrell, Thomas. *Norms of Rhetorical Culture.* New Haven: Yale University Press, 1993.

Fest, Joachim. "Encumbered Remembrance: The Controversy about the Incomparability of National Socialist Crimes." In *Forever in the Shadow of Hitler,* translated by J. Knowlton and T. Cates, 63–71. Atlantic Highlands, N.J.: Humanities Press International, 1986.

*Forever in the Shadow of Hitler.* Translated by James Knowlton and Truett Cates. Atlantic Highlands, N.J.: Humanities Press International, 1993.

Foucault, Michel. "A Preface to Transgression." *Critique* 195–96 (1963): 751–70.

———. *The Archaeology of Knowledge.* New York: Pantheon Books, 1972.

———. "The Subject and Power." Afterword to *Michel Foucault: Beyond Structuralism and Hermeneutics,* edited by Hubert Dreyfus and Paul Rabinow. Brighton: Harvester Press, 1982.

———. *The Foucault Reader.* Edited by Paul Rabinow. New York: Pantheon Books, 1984.

Freeman, Alan. "Document Outlines Steps Against Sovereignty." *Globe and Mail,* 21 October 1995: A1+.

Friedländer, Saul. "Some German Struggles with Memory." In *Bitburg in Moral and Political Perspective,* edited by Geoffrey H. Hartman. Bloomington: Indiana University Press, 27–42.

Frolov, A. "About the Real Subject of Market Reforms." *Russian Economic Journal* 1 (1999): 40–50.

Gaebel, Hans-Herbert. "Kein Einzelfall." *Frankfurter Rundschau,* 12 November 1988, A3.

Gagnon, Lysiane. "Triste fin de carrière." *La Presse,* 1 November 1995, B3.

Gamache, Claude. "Two Visions: The Canadian Dilemma." *Winnipeg Free Press*, 30 October 1995, A7.

Garvuzova, Olga. "Kommunopatrioty Zhdali Khasbulatova." *Nezavisimaia Gazeta*, 6 June 1993, 2.

Gellner, Ernest. *Nations and Nationalism*. Oxford: Basil Blackwell, 1983.

Giddens, Anthony. *The Nation-State and Violence*. Cambridge, Mass.: Polity Press, 1985.

Girnth, Heiko. "Einstellung and Einstellungsbekündung in der politischen Rede: Eine sprachwissenschaftliche Untersuchung der Rede Philipp Jenningers vom 10. November 1988." In *Europäische Hochschulschriften*. Frankfurt am Main: Peter Lang, 1993.

Gleason, Gregory. "Nationalism and Its Discontents." *Russian Review* 53 (1993): 79–90.

Goble, Paul A. "Three Faces of Nationalism in the Former Soviet Union." In *Nationalism and Nationalities in the New Europe*, edited by Charles A. Kupchan, 122–35. Ithaca, N.Y.: Cornell University Press, 1995.

Goldhagen, Daniel. *Hitler's Willing Executioners: Ordinary Germans and the Holocaust*. New York: Alfred A. Knopf, 1996.

Goshko, John M. "Yeltsin Receives Widespread Backing for Assault: In the U.S. Victory Seen for Democracy." *Washington Post*, 5 October 1993, A29.

Gougeon, Gilles. *A History of Québec Nationalism*, translated by Louisa Blair, Robert Chodos, and Jane Ubertino. Toronto: James Lorimer & Company, 1994.

Gray, John. *False Dawn*. New York: New Press, 1998.

Greenfield, Liah. *Nationalism: Five Roads to Modernity*. Cambridge, Mass.: Harvard University Press, 1992.

———."The Formation of the Russian National Identity: The Role of Status Insecurity and Ressentiment." *Comparative Studies in Society and History* 32 (1990): 549–91.

Grushin, Boris. Editorial. *Rossijskie Vestie*, 24 March 1993, 1.

Gustafson, Thane. *Capitalism Russian Style*. Cambridge: Cambridge University Press, 1999.

Ha, Tu Thanh. "Bouchard Remarks Spark Outcry: Yes Leader Dismisses Attacks Over 'White Races' Comment as Petty Politicking." *Globe and Mail*, 16 October 1995, A1+.

———. "Bouchard Defends 'White Race' Remark." *Globe and Mail*, 17 October 1995, A1+.

———. "Bouchard Comment Puzzling." *Globe and Mail*, 17 October 1995, A18.

———. "Yes Vote No Picnic, Chrétien Warns." *Globe and Mail*, 19 October 1995, A1+.

Haber, Honi Fern. *Beyond Postmodern Politics*. New York: Routledge, 1994.

Habermas, Jürgen. "A Kind of Settlement of Damages: The Apologetic Tendencies in German History Writing." In *Forever in the Shadow of Hitler*, translated by J. Knowlton and T. Cates, 34–44. Atlantic Highlands, N.J.: Humanities Press International, 1986.

————. "Defusing the Past: A Politico-Cultural Tract." In *Bitburg in Moral and Political Perspective*, edited by Geoffrey H. Hartmann, 43–51. Bloomington: Indiana University Press, 1986.

Hall, Rodney Bruce. *National Collective Identity: Social Constructs and International Systems*. New York: Columbia University Press, 1999.

Hall, Stuart. "Signification, Representation, Ideology: Althusser and the Post-Structuralist Debates." *Critical Studies in Mass Communication* 2 (1985): 94–112.

Handler, Richard. *Nationalism and the Politics of Culture in Québec*. Madison: University of Wisconsin Press, 1988.

Hartmann, Geoffrey, ed. *Bitburg in Moral and Political Perspective*. Bloomington: University of Indiana Press, 1986.

Hedetoft, Ulf. "National Identity and Mentalities of War in Three EC Countries." *Journal of Peace Research* 30 (1993): 281–300.

Herles, Helmut. "Das mildeste Urteil lautet: Gut gemeint, aber nicht gekonnt." *Frankfurter Allgemeine Zeitung*, 11 November 1988, A3.

Hobsbawm, Eric H. *Nations and Nationalism since 1780: Programme, Myth, Reality*. New York: Cambridge University Press, 1990.

Hobsbawm, Eric, and Terrance Ranger, eds. *The Invention of Tradition*. Cambridge: Cambridge University Press, 1983.

Hoffman, Erik P. "Challenges to Viable Constitutionalism in Post-Soviet Russia." *Harriman Review* 7 (1994): 19–56.

Hughes, James. "Regionalism in Russia: The Rise and Fall of the Siberian Agreement." *Europe-Asia Studies* 46, 7 (1994): 1133–61.

Huskey, Eugene. "Democracy and Institutional Design in Russia." *Demokratizatsiya: The Journal of Post-Soviet Democratization* 4 (1996): 461–65.

Hutchinson, John, and Anthony Smith, eds. *Nationalism*. New York: Oxford University Press, 1994.

Janßen, Karl-Heinz. "Die Wahrheit nicht bezweifelt." *Die Zeit*, 18 November 1988, A3.

Jenninger, Philipp. Address. German Bundestag, Fiftieth Anniversary of the *Reichskristallnacht*, Berlin. 10 November 1988. *Die Zeit*, Nr. 47, 25 November 1988.

————. "Von der Verantwortung für das Vergangene." *Die Zeit*, 25 November 1988, A4+.

Jens, Walter. "Ungehaltene Worte über eine gehalten Rede." *Die Zeit*, 18 November 1988, A3.

Jusdanis, Gregory. "Beyond National Culture?" *Boundary* 2 22 (1995): 23–60.

Kaplan, Fred. "Yeltsin Acts to Bolster His Powers." *Boston Globe*, 6 October 1993, A1.

Kedourie, Elie. *Nationalism*. Cambridge, Mass.: Blackwell, 1993.

Khasbulatov, Ruslan. "Verkhovnyi Sovet—Za Konstruktivnoe Sotrudnichestvo." *Rossiskaia Gazeta*, 8 June 1993, 1+.

————. "The President Is Trampling on the Constitution: In the Hour of Trial, Rise to the Defense of Democracy," *Rossiskaya gazeta*, 23 September 1993, 1+.

Kissinger, Henry. *Diplomacy*. New York: Simon & Schuster, 1994.

Kocka, Jürgen. "Hitler Should Not Be Repressed by Stalin and Pol Pot: On the Attempts of German Historians to Relativize the Enormity of the Nazi Crimes." In *Forever in the Shadow of Hitler*, translated by J. Knowlton and T. Cates, 85–92. Atlantic Highlands, N.J.: Humanities Press International, 1986.

Kolesnikova, Andrey. Editorial. *Rossijskie Vestie*, 24 March 1993, 1.

Kukathas, Chandran. "Liberalism, Communitarianism, and Political Community." In *The Communitarian Challenge to Liberalism*, edited by Ellen F. Paul, Fred D. Miller Jr., and Jeffrey Paul, 80–104. Cambridge: Cambridge University Press, 1996.

Kymlicka, Will. "Social Unity in a Liberal State." In *The Communitarian Challenge to Liberalism*, edited by Ellen F. Paul, Fred D. Miller Jr., and Jeffrey Paul, 105–36. Cambridge: Cambridge University Press, 1996.

Laclau, Ernesto, and Chantal Mouffe. *Hegemony and Socialist Strategy: Towards a Radical Democratic Politics*. Translated by Winston Moore and Paul Cammack. New York: Verso, 1985.

LaForest, Guy. "Fraud, Shame and Injustice." *Globe and Mail*, 30 October 1995, A21.

Lahaise, Robert. "Interview with Robert Lahaise." In Gilles Gougeon, ed., *A History of Québec Nationalism*, translated by Louisa Blair, Robert Chodos, and Jane Ubertino, 4–16. Toronto: James Lorimer & Company, 1994.

Lapidus, Gail W., and Edward W. Walker. "Nationalism, Regionalism, and Federalism: Center-Periphery Relations in Post-Communist Russia." In *The New Russia: Troubled Transformation*, edited by Gail W. Lapidus, 79–114. Boulder, Colo.: Westview, 1994.

Lapina, N., and A. Chirikova, "Regionalnye ekonomicheskiye eilty: Mentalitet, povedenie, vzaimodeystviye so vlastiuy." *Obschevestvo I edonomika* 6 (1999): 277.

Legendre, Camille. *French Canada in Crisis: A New Society in the Making?* London: Expedite Graphic Limited, 1980.

Lempert, David. "Changing Russian Political Culture in the 1990s: Parasites, Paradigms, and Perestroika." *Comparative Studies in Society and History* 35 (1993): 628–46.

Lessard, Denis. "Lucien Bouchard S'en Vient." *La Presse*, 1 November 1995, A1+.

Lett, Dan, and Doug Nairne. "Bouchard Vows Quick Return; Parizeau Stuns." *Winnipeg Free Press*, 31 October 1995, A1+.

Linkov, Aleksandr. "Uidet Predstavitelnaia Vlast—Pridet Diktatura." *Rossiiskaia Gazeta*, 8 June 1993, 2.

Mackie, Richard. "Bouchard Berated at Rally of 3,000 Federalist Women." *Globe and Mail*, 28 October 1995, A3.

———. "Yes 50.2, No 49.8, Poll Suggests: Emotional Factors Affect Voters' Decisions as Bouchard's Speeches Galvanize Yes Campaign." *Globe and Mail*, 21 October 1995, A1+.

Maier, Charles S. *The Unmasterable Past: History, Holocaust, and German National Identity*. Cambridge: Harvard University Press, 1988.

McGee, Michael C. "In Search of 'The People': A Rhetorical Alternative." *Quarterly Journal of Speech* 61 (1975): 235–49.

———. "Text, Context, and the Fragmentation of Contemporary Culture." *Western Journal of Speech Communication* 54 (1990): 274–89.

McGee, Michael C., and Martha Anne Martin. "Public Knowledge and Ideological Argumentation." *Communication Monographs* 50 (1983): 47–65.

McKenzie, Donald. "Numerically Speaking, Parizeau May Be Right: Ethnic Vote Pro-No, But Premier's Swipe a No-No." *Winnipeg Free Press*, 1 November 1995, B2.

McKerrow, Raymie E. "Critical Rhetoric: Theory and Praxis." *Communication Monographs* 56 (1989): 91–111.

———. "Argument Communities." In *Perspectives on Argumentation*, edited by Robert Trapp and Janice Schuetz, 27–40. Prospect Heights, Ill.: Waveland Press, 1990.

McManus, Doyle. "Clinton Messages His Support for Yeltsin." *Los Angeles Times*, 12 March 1993, A10.

McManus, Doyle, and Elizabeth Shogrun. "Yeltsin's Defiant Victory." *Los Angeles Times*, 22 August 1991, A1+.

Miner, Steven M. "Yeltsin Is Democrat Enough for His Times." *Newsday*, 7 October 1993, 127.

Miyoshi, Masao. "A Borderless World? From Colonialism to Transnationalism and the Decline of the Nation-State." *Critical Inquiry* 19 (1993): 726–51.

Mörbitz, Eghard. "Eine ausgesprochen deutsche Tragödie." *Frankfurter Rundschau*, 12 November 1988, A3.

Mouffe, Chantal. "Democratic Politics and the Question of Identity." In *The Identity in Question*, edited by John Rajchman, 33–46. New York: Routledge, 1995.

"Mr. Bouchard's Ethnic Nationalism." *Globe and Mail*, 17 October 1995: A18.

Müller, Heiner. "Germany's Identity Crisis." *New Perspectives Quarterly* 10 (1993): 16–19.

Nairn, Doug. "Dream Dies, Crowd Weeps." *Winnipeg Free Press*, 31 October 1995, A1+.

Neumann, Iver B. *Russia and the Idea of Europe: A Study in Identity and International Relations.* New York: Routledge, 1996.

Nietzsche, Friedrich. "On Truth and Lie in an Extra-Moral Sense." In *Philosophy and Truth: Selections From Nietzsche's Notebooks of the Early 1970s.* Translated and edited by Daniel Breazeale. Atlantic Highlands, N.J.: Humanities Press, 1979.

———. *On the Advantage and Disadvantage of History for Life.* Indianapolis, Ind.: Hacket, 1980.

Nikitinskii, Leonid. "We Still Have a Choice Between Two Democracies." *Izvestia*, 23 September 1993, 3.

Nolte, Ernst. "The Past That Will Not Pass: A Speech That Could Be Written but Not Delivered." *Forever in the Shadow of Hitler*, translated by J. Knowlton and T. Cates, 18–23. Atlantic Highlands, N.J.: Humanities Press International, 1986.

Nonnenmacher, Günther. "Der Umgang mit unserer Geschichte." *Frankfurter Allgemeine Zeitung*, 12 November 1988, A1.

"Obraschenie presidenta RF k grazhdanam rossii I otvet emu chitatelei pravdy." *Pravda*, 24 March 1993, 1+.

"Obrashchenie K Grazhdanam Rossiiskoi Federatsii." *Pravda* 8 June 1993: 1.

Olson, Kathryn. "The Controversy Over President Reagan's Visit to Bitburg: Strategies of Definition and Redefinition." *Quarterly Journal of Speech* 75 (1989): 129–51.

———. "The Function of Form in Newspapers' Political Coverage: The New York Times' Shaping of Expectations in the Bitburg Controversy." *Political Communication* 12 (1995): 46–64.

Ouimet, Michèle. "Les Francophones ont aussie aidé le NON." *La Presse*, 1 November 1995, B8.

Parizeau, Jacques. "Address for the Inauguration of the National Yes Committee, 7 October 1995." *Parti Québécois* homepage. http://198.168.84.30/en/idees/disc/dj071095.html (11 July 1996).

———. "Address to Yes Supporters on the Evening of the 1995 Referendum's Defeat." Canadian Broadcasting Corporation, 30 October 1995.

"Parliament Ousts Yeltsin, Names Rutskoi President." *Current Digest of the Post-Soviet Press* 45, 38 (1993): 4–5.

Parti Québécois homepage. http://198.168.84/30/en/gens/chefs (July 1996).

Pavlov, Nikolau. "Yeltsin's Fiasco—A Slap on the Cheek—On the Results of the Eighth Congress of the People's Deputies of Russia." *Den'*, 21–28 March 1993, 1.

Perelman, Chaim. *The New Rhetoric*. Notre Dame, Ind.: University of Notre Dame Press, 1969.

Perlamutrov, Vilan. "Toward a Market Economy or Toward Economic Catastrophe?" *Problems of Economic Transition* (1994): 24–40.

Pipes, Richard. *The Formation of the Soviet Union*. Cambridge, Mass.: Harvard University Press, 1997.

Polenz, Peter. "Verdünnte Sprachkulture: Das Jenninger-Syndrom in sprachkritischer Sicht." *Deutsche Sprache* 4 (1989): 289–316.

"Radio Parliament' Rallies to the Defence of Khasbulatov." *BBC Summary of World Broadcasts*, 9 June 1993.

Rajchman, John, ed. *The Identity in Question*. New York: Routledge, 1995.

Reifenrath, Roderich. "Warum mußte er reden?" *Frankfurter Rundschau*, 11 November 1988, A3.

Rigby, T. H. "Conclusion: Russia in Search of Its Future." In *Russia in Search of Its Future*, edited by Amin Saikal and William Maley, 207–25. Cambridge: Cambridge University Press, 1995.

Ringmar, Erik. "Nationalism: The Idiocy of Intimacy," *British Journal of Sociology* 49 (1998): 534–49.

Rioux, Marcel. "The Development of Ideologies in Quebec." In *A Passion for Identity*, edited by Eli Mandel and David Taras, 267–88. Agincourt, Ont.: Methuen, 1987.

Robbins, Carla Anne, Gary Fields, and Steven Liesman. "U.S. Plans to File Suit Against Harvard Over Its Russian Foreign Aid Program." *Wall Street Journal*, 26 September 2000, A4.

Rodriguez, George. "Empty Victory." *Fort Lauderdale Sun Sentinel*, 10 October 1993, G1.

Rywkin, Michael. *Moscow's Lost Empire*. New York: M. E. Sharpe, 1994.

Sakharov, Nikolia. "The President Must Have a Right to Dissolve the Parliament." *Rossiskaia gazeta*, 23 September 1993, 2.

Sakwa, Richard. *Russian Politics and Society*. New York: Routledge, 1993.

Sapov, Viktor. "Demokratiia Pod Bashmakom Prezidenta. V. Chechne—Pod Gusenitsami Tankov." *Pravda*, 8 June 1993, 1+.

Scheer, Robert. "Giving Yeltsin a Blank Check Is Disastrous." *Los Angeles Times*, 5 November 1993, B7.

Scheuerman, William E. "Globalization and Exceptional Powers: The Erosion of Liberal Democracy." *Radical Philosophy* (January 1999): 1–18.

Schöpflin, George. "National Identity in the Soviet Union and East Central Europe." *Ethnic and Racial Studies* 14 (1991): 3–14.

Sennet, Richard. *The Fall of Public Man*. New York: W. W. Norton, 1977.

Seton-Watson, Hugh. *Nations and States: An Enquiry into the Origins of Nations and the Politics of Nationalism*. Boulder, Colo.: Westview Press, 1977.

Sharlet. Robert. "Russia's 'Ethnic' Republics and Constitutional Politics." *Eurasian Reports* 3 (1993): 39–46.

———. "Russian Constitutional Crisis: Law and Politics Under Yeltsin," *Post-Soviet Affairs* 9 (1993): 314–36.

———. "The Prospects for Federalism in Russian Constitutional Politics." *Publius* 24, 2 (1994): 115–27.

———. "The New Russian Constitution and Its Political Impact." *Problems of Post-Communism* 42 (1995): 3–7.

Shevtsova, Lilia. "Russia's Post-Communist Politics: Revolution or Continuity." In *The New Russia: Troubled Transformation*, edited by Gail W. Lapidus, 5–36. Boulder, Colo.: Westview Press, 1995.

Shotter, John, and Kenneth J. Gergen, eds. *Texts of Identity*. London: Sage Publications, 1989.

Simes, Dimitri. "Testing Yeltsin's Authoritarian Reflexes." *Washington Post*, 6 October 1991, C1.

Simons, Jon. *Foucault and the Political*. New York: Routledge, 1995.

Sloop, John M., and Kent Ono. "Out-law Discourse: The Critical Politics of Material Judgement." *Philosophy and Rhetoric* 30 (1997): 50–69.

Smith, Anthony. *National Identity*. Las Vegas: University of Nevada Press, 1991.

———. *Nations and Nationalism in a Global Era*. Cambridge, Mass.: Polity Press, 1995.

Smith, Graham. "Mapping the Federal Condition: Ideology, Political Practice and Social Justice." In *Federalism: The Multiethnic Challenge*, edited by Graham Smith, 1–28. New York: Longman, 1995.

"Statement by the Russian Government." *Izvestia*, 23 March 1993, 1.

Steele, Jonathan. "The President Who Would Become Tsar." *London Guardian*, 3 June 1993, 9.

Stinson, Marian. "Dollar Plunges on Fears of Yes Vote." *Globe and Mail*, 21 October 1995, A1+.

Stürmer, Michael. "History in a Land Without History." In *Forever in the Shadow of Hitler*, translated by J. Knowlton and T. Cates, 16–17. Atlantic Highlands, N.J.: Humanities Press International, 1986.

———. "An Indictment That Fabricates Even Its Sources." In *Forever in the Shadow of Hitler*, translated by J. Knowlton and T. Cates, 61–62. Atlantic Highlands, N.J.: Humanities Press International, 1986.

———"How Much History Weighs." In *Forever In the Shadow of Hitler*, translated by J. Knowlton and T. Cates. 196-97. Atlantic Highlands, N.J.: Humanities Press International, 1986.

Suny, Ronald G. *The Revenge of the Past: Nationalism, Revolution, and the Collapse of the Soviet Union*. Stanford: Stanford University Press, 1993.

Szporluk, Roman. *Communism and Nationalism: Karl Marx versus Friedrich List*. New York: Oxford University Press, 1988.

Tarlton, Charles D. "Symmetry and Asymmetry as Elements of Federalism: A Theoretical Speculation." *Journal of Politics* 27 (1965): 861–74.

Taylor, Charles. *Sources of the Self: The Making of the Modern Identity*. Cambridge: Cambridge University Press, 1989.

———. *Multiculturalism: Examining the Politics of Recognition*. Edited by Amy Gutman. Princeton, N.J.: Princeton University Press, 1994.

Teague, Elizabeth. "Center-Periphery Relations in the Russian Federation." In *National Identity and Ethnicity in Russia and the New States of Eurasia*, edited by Roman Szporluk, 21–57. New York: M. E. Sharpe, 1994.

Thongchai, Winichakul. *Siam Mapped: A History of the Geo-Body of a Nation*. Honolulu: Hawaii University Press, 1994.

Tolstyh, Valentin. Editorial. *Nezavisimaia Gazeta*, 23 March 1993, 3.

Tolz, Vera. "Power Struggle in Russia: The Role of the Republics and Regions." *RFE/RL Research Report*, 9 April 1993, 8–13.

———. "Drafting the New Russian Constitution." *RFE/RL Research Report* vol. 2, issue 29, 16 July 1993, 9.

Tretyakov, Vitaly. "Don't Make Any More Mistakes." *Nezavisimaia Gazeta*, 23 March 1993, 1.

Trudeau, Pierre Elliot. *Pierre Trudeau Speaks Out on Meech Lake*. Toronto: General Paperbacks, 1990.

Trushkov, Victor. *Pravda* 8 June 1993: 1.

Tucker, Robert C. "Post-Soviet Leadership and Change." In *Patterns in Post-Soviet Leadership*, edited by Timothy J. Colton and Robert C. Tucker, 5–28. Boulder, Colo.: Westview Press, 1995.

Urban, Michael. "National Conflict Internalized: A Discourse Analysis of the Fall of the First Russian Republic." In *The Myth of 'Ethnic Conflict': Politics, Economics, and 'Cultural Violence,'* edited by Beverly Crawford and Ronnie D. Lipschutz, 108–46. Berkeley: University of California Press, 1998.

Walker, Edward. "Moscow and the Provinces: Economic and Political Dimensions of Russian Regionalism." *Eurasian Reports* 3 (1993): 47–64.

———. "The New Russian Constitution and the Future of the Russian Federation." *Harriman Institute Forum* 5 (1992): 10–11.

Wallerstein, Immanuel. "Class Conflict in the Capitalist World-Economy." In *Race, Nation, Class: Ambiguous Identities*, translated by Chris Turner, 115–24. New York: Verso, 1991.

Ward, Olivia. "Russian Talks on Constitution Off to Rocky Start." *Toronto Star*, 6 June 1993, A2.

Wedel, Janine R. *Collision and Collusion: The Strange Case of Western Aid to Eastern Europe.* New York: Palgrave, 2001.

Weizsäcker, Richard von. "Speech to the Bundestag During the Ceremony Commemorating the 40th Anniversary of the End of the War in Europe and of National Socialist Tyranny, May 8, 1985." In *Bitburg in Moral and Political Perspective*, translated and edited by Geoffrey H. Hartmann, 262–73. Bloomington: Indiana University Press, 1986.

West, Cornel. "A Matter of Life and Death." In *The Identity in Question*, edited by John Rajchman, 15–32. New York: Routledge, 1995.

White, Hayden. "Historical Emplotment and the Problem of Truth." In *Probing the Limits of Representation: Nazism and the 'Final Solution,'* edited by Saul Friedlander, 37–44. Cambridge, Mass.: Harvard University Press, 1992.

Williams, Colin H. "A Requiem for Canada?" *Federalism: The Multiethnic Challenge*, edited by Graham Smith, 31–72. Longman: New York, 1995.

Winkler, Heinrich A. "Eternally in the Shadow of Hitler? The Dispute about the Germans' Understanding of History." In *Forever in the Shadow of Hitler*, translated by J. Knowlton and T. Cates, 171–76. Atlantic Highlands, N.J.: Humanities Press International, 1986.

"Yeltsin's Victory Seen as a Boost for Democracy," *Congressional Record*, 7 October 1993, A33.

Yeltsin, Boris. "Yeltsin's Inaugural Address." *Dow Jones Interactive Library* (Online), *Dow Jones News Retrieval*, 10 July 1991.

———. "Opening Speech to the Constitutional Assembly." *BBC Summary of World Broadcasts*, 7 June 1993, 63–71.

———. "On the Step by Step Constitutional Reform of the Russian Federation." *Dow Jones Interactive Library* (Online), *Dow Jones News Retrieval*, 21 September 1993.

———. "On the Step by Step Constitutional Reform of the Russian Federation." *Current Digest of the Post-Soviet Press*, 45, 38 (20 October 1993): 1.

———. *The Struggle for Russia.* Translated by Catherine A. Fitzpatrick. New York: Belka, 1994.

# INDEX

Russia (*continued*)
    crisis, 33–34, 111n. 4; privatization,
    48, 64, 118n. 125; public sphere, 3,
    44; referendums, 48, 52; regional
    republics, 52, 113nn. 19, 27; rule by
    executive decree, 35–38, 44–52; sepa-
    ration of powers, 41–42, 44–45, 64;
    "Soviets," characterization of, 35, 44,
    49, 53–56; strategies of remembrance,
    7–10, 35, 44–45, 53–56; territorial
    principle, 42–43; U.S. characteriza-
    tion of, 10, 34–35, 50, 61–62, 64–66,
    100; weakness of, 64, 117n. 118. *See
    also* Russian constitution
Russian constitution: alternative drafts,
    43–44; battle over, 41–45; Brezhnev-
    era constitution, 53, 55; constitution
    of 1993, 37–38, 64; constitutional
    battle, 41–45; post-coup develop-
    ments, 62–63; presidential version,
    52, 58; Soviet-era constitution,
    35–36, 54–55, 79. *See also* Russia
Rutskoi, Alexander, 49, 50, 60–61,
    115n. 54

Sakwa, Richard, 65
Scheuerman, William E., 66
self-determination, 39–40
Shakhrai, Sergei, 43
Simes, Dmitri, 62–63
situational theory, 91, 98
Slobodkin, Yuri, 53, 57
Sloop, John M., 105n. 25
Smith, Anthony, 91, 94–95
Sobchak, Anatoly, 43
sovereignty, 41, 98
Soviet Union, 22, 79; collapse, 33, 43,
    44; constitution, 35–36, 54–55, 79;
    nationalities problem, 38–41;
    Supreme Soviet, 52, 114n. 40
Stalin, Joseph, 39–40

state, 5–6; economic motives, 69–70, 98.
    *See also* nation-state
state representatives, 1, 13, 69, 97
strategies of remembrance, 3, 104n. 7;
    analysis of controversial discourse,
    7–9, 89, 93–94, 101, 120n. 24;
    civic/economic dimensions of
    national identity, 6, 17, 56, 77–81,
    95–96; claims of "truth," 50–56, 80,
    82; colonial rhetoric, 70–73, 77,
    80–81, 85; confusion of, 28–30; con-
    servatives *vs.* critics, 16–17, 24,
    28–30, 108n. 39; dissociations, 46–47;
    forgetting, 7–8, 14–15, 93; impropri-
    ety of discourse, 25–26, 93; mapping,
    6–9; narrative absences, 7, 9, 31–32,
    90, 92, 94–95, 106n. 30, 117n. 116;
    rhetorical strategies, 1–2, 7, 44–45,
    80–81, 89; shifts in, 10, 80, 83–86,
    95; strategic multiculturalism, 8, 10,
    85–88, 94, 98, 100; transgression of
    limits, 7, 12, 19, 23, 25, 29–30, 100
strategy (as term), 106n. 31
Strauss, Joseph, 16
Stürmer, Michael, 16
subjunctive form, 27
Supreme Soviet, 52, 114n. 40

Talbott, Strobe, 36, 50, 65, 67
Taylor, Charles, 87
*Tendenzwende*, 15–16
territorial principle, 42–43
totalitarianism, 96, 99–100
Tretyakov, Vitaly, 49
Trotsky, Leon, 94
Trudeau, Pierre, 77, 78–79, 120n. 31
Trushkov, Victor, 58

United States: characterization of Russia
    as democratic, 10, 34–35, 50, 61–62,
    64–66, 100; characterization of West

German victims, 9, 10, 13–15; political goals, 14–15
Urban, Michael, 44

violence, 89
Voronin, Yuri, 49

Walker, Edward, 38–39, 63
Wallerstein, Immanuel, 69, 81–82, 98
*Washington Post,* 61
Weisäcker, Richard von, 10, 12, 14, 16, 18–24, 26, 29, 33, 100; central themes, 20–21
West, Cornel, 69
West Germany, 4, 7, 9, 12–13, 69, 95; audiences in position of perpetrators, 25–26, 28, 29, 110n. 59; commemorative discourse, 18–19, 20; economic concerns, 17–18, 97; forgetting, 31–32; healthy national consciousness, 17–19; *Historikerstreit,* 13, 15–19, 29, 32; media, 19–20, 25; minimization of responsibility, 3, 14–17, 21–23, 92, 100; national identity, 13, 18–19, 95; perpetrators as victims, 21, 25–26, 28; remembrance for reunification, 19–24, 109n. 43; remembrance of National Socialism, 13–19; *Tendenzwende,* 15–16; victims, discourse of, 7, 15, 17–18, 21–22, 32, 69, 92, 108n. 36; victims, expansion of categories, 23–24, 108n. 37; Weisäcker speech and, 19–24; younger generation, 12, 16, 30, 111n. 68. *See also* Jenninger, Philipp; National Socialism; Weisäcker, Richard von
Western national identities, 95–96

Yeltsin, Boris, 7, 10, 79; attack on Supreme Soviet, 59–60; as autocrat, 37, 49–50, 52, 56, 62–63; characterization as democratic, 33, 34, 36–37, 47–48, 93, 100; Constitutional Commission and, 43–44; constitutional coup, 36–37, 58–61; inaugural address (July, 1991), 36; media reactions to speeches, 37, 49–51, 56–57, 60–61; press conferences, 60–61; rule by executive decree, 35–38, 44; speech of 5 June, 1993, 34–35, 52–58; speech of 20 March, 1993, 34, 38; speech of 23 September, 1993, 35, 45–52; stripped of power, 45, 61
Yes Supporters, 84

Zorkin, Valery, 49, 50, 57, 60, 61, 115n. 54